HISTORICAL RECORD

2ND (NOW 80TH), OR

Royal Tyrone Fusilier Regiment of Militia,

From the Embodiment in 1793 to the Present Time.

BY

QUARTERMASTER JOHN CORE.

1872.

INSCRIBED

TO THE MEMORY OF

J A M E S D u P R É A L E X A N D E R ,

SECOND

EARL OF CALEDON,

COLONEL OF THE ROYAL TYRONE FUSILIER

REGIMENT OF MILITIA,

TO WHOM THE AUTHOR IS INDEBTED FOR

MANY ACTS OF KINDNESS,

AND HIS PRESENT HONORABLE POSITION

IN THE REGIMENT.

CHAPTER V.   PAGE.

CONTENTS.

CHAPTER I.

PREFACE.

As no record of the history of the Royal Tyrone Regiment of Militia has ever been written, and as enquiry has been frequently made for such a record by generals and inspecting field-officers, at the request of Lieutenant-Colonel James A. Caulfeild, commandant of the regiment, I undertook the task of compiling one, but not without many misgivings as to my ability to do justice to the history of this corps, with which I have been identified for almost fifty-nine years. It has given me peculiar pleasure in my researches amongst the old regimental books to have brought to my recollection persons and incidents which had altogether passed from my mind. I can recall many a long and weary march—I can see well, and recognize the features of the officers, from many of whom I received attention and kindness even when a boy—I can almost hear the familiar voices of my old comrades ; but this pleasure is not unmixed with pain, when I consider that all these have passed away, and that I remain alone the last man of the old regiment.

The toil that I have had in preparing this record will be amply repaid if I have succeeded in enlisting the interest of the reader in behalf of a regiment which was always second to none in loyalty, good conduct, and soldier-like appearance, and always foremost in readiness to serve the Crown and country.

J. C.

Omagh, January, 1872.

LIST OF OFFICERS.

Headquarters—Strabane, 1793.

Rank.		Name.	Date of Commission.
Lieut.-Colonel Commandant, }		The Marquis of Abercorn,	1793.
Lieut.-Colonel,	—	The Hon. Thomas Knox,	May 18, 1793.
Major,	—	The Hon. A. C. Hamilton,	,,
Captain,	—	Benjamain Stewart, —	,,
,,	—	Charles Crawford, —	May 19, 1793.
,,	—	Alexander Richardson, —	May 20, 1793.
,,	—	John Mackay, —	May 21, 1793.
,,	—	John Moutray, —	May 22, 1793.
,,	—	George Gledstanes, —	May 23, 1793.
,,	—	Richard Dobbins,* —	May 24, 1793.
Lieutenants,	—	George Vallancy,† —	May 25, 1793.
,,	—	Andrew Thomas Bell, —	May 26, 1793.
,,	—	George Sinclair, —	May 27, 1793.
,,	—	Thomas Spillar, —	,,
,,	—	William Goodlatte, —	,,
,,	—	Thomas Lawrence, —	,,
,,	—	Claude Walsh, —	,,
,,	—	William Lighton, —	,,
,,	—	Joseph Crump, —	,,
,,	—	James Taylor, —	,,
Ensigns,	—	James Vernon, —	,,
,,	—	Michael Richardson, —	,,
,,	—	David Campbell, —	,,
,,	—	William Hamilton, —	May 28, 1793.
,,	—	Thomas Hamilton, —	,,
,,	—	Hon. Du Pré Alexander,—	,,
,,	—	Lord Viscount Hamilton,	May 29, 1793.
,,	—	Alexander Anderson, —	May 31, 1793.
Chaplain,	—	Rev. Stewart Hamilton,—	May 28, 1793.

* Appointed Quartermaster, 23rd August 1793.
† Brevet Captain and Adjutant.

CHAPTER I.

ORIGINAL WARRANT FOR EMBODYING THE TYRONE REGIMENT OF MILITIA.

By the Lord Lieutenant General and General Governor of Ireland.

WESTMORELAND,

In pursuance of the powers vested in us by the Act for amending and reducing into one Act of Parliament the laws relating to the Militia of this kingdom, We are hereby pleased to direct and require you to draw out and embody with all convenient speed the Militia of the County of Tyrone. You are therefore hereby required to do all manner of things which by the said Act are in this case made and provided for the drawing out and embodying of the said Militia accordingly. And for so doing this shall be your Warrant. Given at His Majesty's Castle of Dublin this 18th day of July, 1793.

By His Excellency's command,

To the Most Noble   R. HOBAT.
  The Marquis of Abercorn,
    Lieutenant-Colonel Commandant,
And the Governors of the County of Tyrone.

Strabane, 23rd August, 1793.

" The Parliament of this kingdom having passed a law for raising and embodying a Militia for the defence thereof, and His Majesty King George the Third, through His Excellency the Lord Lieutenant of Ireland, having been pleased to appoint the Most Noble the Marquis of Abercorn to be Lieutenant-

B

Colonel Commandant of the regiment to be raised and embodied in the County of Tyrone, the Marquis of Abercorn, therefore, takes on himself this day the command of the said regiment.

"His Majesty has been graciously pleased to permit the Tyrone Regiment to be called 'Royal.' It is therefore to be known by the name of the '2nd, or Royal Tyrone Regiment of Militia'"—which name it bore up to the year 1855.

As Colonel Commandant, the Marquis was vested with the authority and privilege of appointing all the officers who were to hold commissions in his regiment. These were required to be gentlemen of the County, or to have property therein, and it is evident to anyone acquainted with the County Tyrone that the Marquis's selection of the officers to serve in the Royal Tyrone Regiment was the very best which could have been made, as he well knew the respectability, standing, and efficiency of the gentlemen whose names are recorded in the foregoing list.

The regiment originally, as at present, consisted of ten companies, three of which were known as the Marquis's, the Colonel's, and the Major's companies.

7th September, 1793.—The pay of the non-commissioned officers, drummers, and privates at this time had been arranged in the following order as regards the amount, and daily issue, and the growing arrears due to the men were to be settled and paid them every two months.

	Full Pay.		Daily Subsistence.	
	s.	D.	s.	D.
Sergeant Major, ...	1	7½	... 1	7½
Quartermaster Sergeant,	1	7½	... 1	7½
Sergeants, ...	1	1½	... 1	0
Corporals, ...	0	10½	... 0	9
Drummers, ...	0	9½	... 0	8
Privates, ...	0	7½	... 0	6

It would appear that the regiment had been only partially supplied with arms and accoutrements at this time, as I find in my research that on the 23rd of September, 1793, a corporal's guard, consisting of himself and six men, were served out with seven firelocks, which he was to deliver over to the new guard in good order and clean. I also find an order dated 28th September, which now-a-days would be considered a rather amusing one—it is this :—" Commanding officers of companies will give particular orders to their men this evening that their hairs are well combed, and the sides and foretop pomatumed, and the tails uniformly tied close to the head. As the men will appear powdered at the review, the officers will be particularly careful on this point, and the old sergeants very attentive to instruct their men."

1st December, 1793.—" The regiment will receive from the quartermaster's stores knapsacks for their present effectives, and as recruits join the regiment, the commanding officers of companies signing receipts for the quartermaster. The men are to be charged 6s. 6d. for each knapsack according to His Majesty's regulations. The Marquis of Abercorn will pay the remainder himself, and when each man's time of service is expired he will receive payment for the knapsack from his successor, according to a valuation of its then state."

23rd January, 1794.—" Each of the battalion companies will furnish one man to practice at the cannon exercise under the orders of Lieut. Leighton. He is to be taken from the rear rank, and to be two months in the regiment."

3rd February, 1794.—"A greater attention must be paid to the tying and powdering of the men's hair. The powder must be better mixed in the hair, and the mark of the teeth of the comb appear on the back of the head, and on the club, by drawing the comb downwards on the hair. Great attention must be paid not to have the powder laid on in clots."

7th February, 1794.—" One man from each of the right battalion companies to be added to the artillery detachment, to be taken from the rear rank. Such as volunteer the duty to be preferred."

17th February, 1794.—"The officers are informed that the Marquis of Abercorn has approved of a hat at Ferris's, Ormond Quay, Dublin, and such as may want will be supplied there any time, agreeable to the one fixed on. Lieut.-Colonel Knox has also sent his breastplate and sword as a pattern to Archer, sword cutler, Essex Bridge, Dublin. Such officers as want these articles can be supplied by applying to Mr. Archer."

4th March, 1794.—"The officers of the Royal Tyrone Regiment return their thanks to the men of the regiment for the alacrity with which they turned out yesterday when the drum beat to arms. Their peaceable and good conduct during the day requires from their officers every expression of gratitude. The marked disapprobation shown by the men at the improper conduct of a few deluded and unthinking men of a neighbouring regiment of militia reflects the highest praise on the Tyrone Regiment. Captain Richardson wants words to express his feelings on this occasion, which has happened during his temporary command of the regiment. He has not failed in making the proper representation of the good conduct of the soldiers to their friend, father, and colonel, the Marquis of Abercorn, to the Government of this kingdom. and to the field officers of the regiment. A gratuity, therefore, of half-a-crown will be paid to each private out of the funds of the regiment, in order to purchase a pair of trousers for each, so that every man may have three good pair. The sergeants of companies will be careful that this money is applied to the above purpose."

On the 5th March, 1794, a meeting was held in Strabane by the provost, burgesses and inhabitants, at which the following resolution was passed :—

" Resolved unanimously, That the hearty thanks of this meeting be returned to the soldiers of the Royal Tyrone Regiment, quartered in this town, for their steady and manly conduct yesterday, when their attachment to their duty, their military obligations, and to their officers, were brought to the test, in consequence of the criminal and highly improper behaviour of the militia of a neighbouring county. Resolved, That as the manner in which they acquitted themselves on this interesting occasion merits praise, and must be highly grateful to themselves on reflection, being an example to every soldier of that regard which he ought to pay to his duty at all times, and more especially on similar occasions.

" Resolved unanimously, That the commanding officer be requested to communicate the above resolutions to the Royal Tyrone Regiment, at this evening parade.—James Hamilton, Provost."

9th March, 1794.—" Lieutenant Colonel Knox assumes the command of the regiment at this time with particular pleasure, after the recent exemplary and most spirited conduct exhibited by the the men, and he desires to express to them his warmest satisfaction for the loyalty and good conduct displayed by them on every occasion, which cannot fail to endear them to their Sovereign, and to increase, if possible, the attachment of their officers. He has the pleasure to announce to them that the public service requiring a regiment of their description to move to the southward, they are to march shortly to the County of Waterford, and he is happy to inform them that it is one of the most plentiful and healthy quarters in the kingdom, and it must be highly flattering to the Royal Tyrone Regiment that His Majesty is pleased to show this strong mark of his confidence in them, in thus placing them in a situation where they will have the honour probably of being the first to resist our enemies the French, in case they should be so hardy as to put their threats of an invasion in execution."

On the 15th of March, the new arms supplied to the regiment were issued to the different companies, but only to such men as were able to march with the regiment, and on Monday, the 17th of March, the entire regiment left Strabane on the route for New Geneva and Waterford. It appears that after the first day's march, the regiment was to break into the following three divisions, namely—

1st Division.	2nd Division.	3rd Division.
Grenadiers,	Capt. Mackay's,	Capt. Stewart's,
Lt.-Colonel's,	Capt. Dobbin's,	Captain Baillie's,
Major's, and	and	and
Capt. Crawford's	Marquis's	Light Infantry
Companies.	Companies.	Companies.

Unfortunately, at this early period of militia life, long marches with heavy knapsacks and pouches well filled with ball cartridge were anything but pleasant. Not so now, from the convenience afforded by the railways for the conveyance of troops from one station to another, which is a great boon to the soldier, as he is neither foot-sore nor weary of the heavy burden of a knapsack. The regiment, it appears, did not reach its new quarters in Waterford until the month of April, and Capt. Mackay's, Capt. Dobbin's, and Capt, Moutray's companies did not leave Waterford for New Geneva until the 23rd of May. An alteration having taken place in the establishment of the regiment at this time by an increase in the number of men, the grenadier company was to consist in future of 3 sergeants, 3 corporals, 2 drummers, 2 fifers, and 47 privates; the light company, 3 sergeants, 3 corporals, 2 drummers, and 47 privates; and each of the other companies, 3 sergeants, 3 corporals, 2 drummers, and 48 privates.

On the 4th of June, being the anniversary of His Majesty's birthday, the Royal Tyrone Regiment fired a royal salute from their battalion guns, and three volleys in answer to the guns from Duncannon Fort.

On the 15th June the following order was issued:—" The regiment to parade to-morrow at ten o'clock, precisely, and at twelve they will fire three volleys and three rounds from the battalion guns, in answer to the guns from Duncannon Fort, on account of the glorious successes of His Majesty's fleet under Lord Howe, who has taken six ships of the line, of 74 and 80 guns each, and sunk two others."

Although several changes had taken place among the captains and subaltern officers of the regiment since its embodiment, I did not notice them, because I did not think it necessary on account of its being little more than a year embodied ; but now that an important change had taken place by the resignation of a field officer, I deem it worthy of being remarked. Lieut.-Colonel the Hon. Thomas Knox having resigned his commission, the Marquis of Abercorn appointed Nathaniel Montgomery Moore, Esq., to be Lieut.-Colonel, whose commission as such was dated the 1st of June, 1794.

The following is an extract taken from the regimental orders of the 3rd August, 1794. "The Lieut.-Colonel observes, notwithstanding the number of cautions given, that the men going to mass of a Sunday, continue the shameful practice of running out of the chapel and getting drunk. Such a disgraceful practice obliges him to take some necessary measures to stop it ; and he trusts this caution will be sufficient to prevent him taking severe ones. He will, in the first instance, represent their conduct to the priest, and if contrary to his admonitions it is continued, he will not allow any men to go to mass at all, but keep them locked up in the barracks while the rest of the men are at their worship." A week previous to the regiment leaving Waterford for Galway, it was reviewed by Major General Craig, whose very flattering approbation of the appearance and good discipline of the regiment, was conveyed by Colonel Moore to the men, and was so pleasing to him, that he said it would be the highest gratification possible to the Marquis of Abercorn to know the result of the review yesterday. A rather amusing order was given in connection with the review a day or two before it took place—it is this :—"The guard on the Reviewing General on Thursday to consist of two tallest and handsomest men from each company of the battalion—Barron and Collins, of the Grenadiers ; Todd, of Captain Stewart's ; Reilly and Gallagher, of Captain Crawford's ; and M'Avoy, of the Colonel's ; Sergeant Core, and Corporal M'Causland, the guard."

The regiment next proceeded to Galway in two divisions, as follows :—

1st Division.	2nd Division.
Grenadiers,	The Marquis's,
Lieut.-Colonel's,	Captain Stewart's,
Captain Bailie's,	Captain Moutray's,
Captain Crawford's, and	Major's, and
Captain Sinclair's	Captain Dobbin's
Companies.	Companies.

The baggage was conveyed by water from Passage to Clonmel. I should have previously observed that on the march from Strabane to Waterford the men were daily supplied with refreshments by the officers in charge of the several divisions, out of a fund raised from men ballotted, but not willing to serve in the regiment; and also that at Christmas prior to their removal the Marquis of Abercorn directed that each volunteer should receive a crown out of this fund. But at the time of the regiment leaving Waterford for Galway, the state of the fund not being sufficient to warrant a regular allowance to the men, it was left in the power of the officer commanding each division to give them some refreshment on the day of a long march, or in bad weather.

On the arrival of the regiment at Galway, Lieut.-Colonel Moore was informed that the water in this town, if taken at improper places, was bad, and that some particular fish were supposed to be very unhealthy. The following is an extract taken from the orders of the 3rd September :—" The soldiers will therefore, for their own sake, be careful on these two points—all water below the bridge is bad, and that made use of should be taken up at low water, and as high up the river as possible. The fish called a ' Black Pollock ' is forbid as much as possible." It is evident from this order how anxious Lieut.-Colonel Moore was for the preservation of the health of the men of the regiment. On the 6th of September, a detachment consisting of 1 sergeant, 1 corporal, and 12 men was ordered to Oughterard for the care and protection of the barracks there ; and on the 10th, 1 subaltern, 2 sergeants, 2 corporals, 1 drummer, and 50 privates were sent to Tuam until the last of the month. From the arrival of the regiment in Galway up to the 16th of September the men appear to have been on billet, as on that day an order was issued for the occupation of the several barracks by the companies, in the following manner, namely :—the Grenadiers, Marquis's, Captain Dobbin's, and Captain Sinclair's, the Shamble Barracks ; Captain Stewart's and Captain Crawford's, the Castle Barracks ; and the Major's, Captain Bailie's, and Captain Moutray's, the Lombard Barracks. From the precautions used at this time, it is most evident that a sudden attack by the French was feared on some part of the Irish coast, else such an order as the following would have been unnecessary :—" In case of any alarm in the night, immediately on the drum beating to arms the companies will parade in their respective squares, two deep, and the commanding officer of each barrack will send an officer to the

commanding officer of the regiment for further orders. The
ammunition boxes to be in such a place that the ammunition
may be given to the men in the night without confusion. The
artillery that arrived yesterday to be parked in the Castle Barrack yard, along with the battalion guns of the Royal Tyrone
Regiment—Corporal Drudge of the artillery to have the general
care and attention of the whole. In case of any alarm, the
men of the Royal Artillery, together with the gunners of the
regiment will parade in the Castle Barracks, and the whole of
the artillery will then be under the command of Lieut. Bell,
who will send for orders to the commanding officer of the regiment." The following is an extract taken from the regimental
orders of the 12th December, 1794 :—" The commanding
officer understands the officers' guard room is constantly made
a scene of conviviality and often riot, highly criminal and contrary to all military discipline. It is now particularly forbid,
under penalty of the severest punishment. It is not in the
power of the commanding officer to restrict gentlemen from
scenes of this kind in private, as long as they commit no excess
against the public ; but in the guard room he would be highly
culpable were he to pass over it. The captain on duty will
visit the officers' guard room at unexpected times, and if he
finds any officer disobeying this order he will send him to his
room under an arrest, and apply for another officer to command
the guard."

3rd January, 1795.—Lieut.-Colonel Moore transmitted to
Major Hamilton, then commanding the regiment at Galway,
the following extract of a letter from the Marquis of Abercorn.
" I feel it incumbent on me to remind you, and to beg you to
remind from time to time whoever may be commanding officer
in your absence, that a strict attention is necessary to the
regular and soldierly behaviour of our officers, of whom we
have now many new ones. I hope, therefore, that you and the
commanding officer in your absence will take care that parades
are as regularly and punctually attended, and all the respective duties in the field and at drill as thoroughly learned and
practised as they were when I had the pleasure of commanding
in person. I take it for granted that the correct uniformity of
appearance and dress continues to be duly adhered to.

I am, dear sir, yours, etc.,

ABERCORN."

On receipt of the foregoing from Lieut.-Colonel Moore, the
following appeared in orders :—

" When the Marquis of Abercorn, at such a distance, appears so anxious for the character and credit of the regiment, it would be highly culpable in Major Hamilton, while he commands, not to enforce and expect the strictest compliance with what the Marquis so strenuously requires. He hopes that the officers by a constant attendance on parades, and regular appearance in the uniform of the regiment, will give him an opportunity of reporting to the Marquis that his orders are strictly adhered to."

17th of February, 1795.—" Lieut.-Colonel Moore, having returned to Galway, takes on himself the command of the regiment with peculiar satisfaction, from the exceeding general good conduct of the men during the winter in their present quarters, and which he will not fail to make a proper representation of to the Marquis of Abercorn.

" The future augmentation that is intended in the militia of this kingdom, in consequence of the repeated threats of the enemy to invade it, calls upon the officers commanding regiments for every exertion early in the spring to perfect their established regiments, so that every attention may be turned to make the recruits of some essential service during the approaching summer. Lieut.-Colonel Moore therefore calls on all officers for their assistance, and in particular on the senior officers, so that little as their assistance may be, it will go towards a perfection of the whole, and he trusts that from the diligence of the men, and the attention and activity of the officers, the Royal Tyrone Regiment may be among the first reported ready to take the field the ensuing summer. The first part of his duty will be strictly adhering to the orders of the Marquis of Abercorn ; and after the letter he has so lately written to the regiment, relative to the uniform, dress, and attendance at duty of the officers, Lieut.-Colonel Moore would think himself culpable were he to pass over any inattention in those points. He must therefore insist on a strict compliance. When the duty is done the young officers will have sufficient time for amusement.

" Lieut. Colonel Moore has observed many of the officers' swords in a very broken condition, and he is very sorry to say they have been in this state since quartered in Geneva. The young officers will please to recollect that their swords are for use and ornament, and if by any accident they are broken, every means should be taken to have them mended, and not let them offend the eye of a commanding officer by being in a state of neither use nor ornament. The last day of this month, Lieut.-

Colonel Moore expects to see every officer complete in his regimental appointments."

On the 16th, 17th, and 19th of March, recruiting parties, under the command of Captains Stewart, Sinclair, and Crawford, were sent to Dungannon, Strabane, and Newtownstewart. On the 20th parties were sent on the same duty to Augher and Clogher, under Lieutenant Cluff, and on the 21st, a party to Aughnacloy, to be under the orders of Captain Stewart, stationed at Dungannon, for the augmentation of the regiment above mentioned.

By this augmentation, which was to take place from the 1st of April, 1795, the strength of the regiment was increased to 42 sergeants, 22 drummers, and 700 rank and file ; and not only had Lieut.-Colonel Moore great expectations from the recruiting parties which he had sent out to gather in the numbers required to complete the regiment, by the zeal and activity of the officers and men thus employed on that duty, but he also relied on the men of the regiment, from the account they could give of the treatment they received and the great care taken of them, that by writing to their friends in the county they would prevail on them to join the Royal Tyrone in preference to other regiments of militia, which at that time were beating up in Tyrone, as it appears, in order to complete their old establishment—having failed in their own counties. As an encouragement to the brothers, cousins, and relations of the men now in the regiment, Lieutenant-Colonel Moore "will give to each man who comes up and attests at the regiment, not under the size of 5ft. 6in., a present of one guinea, besides the guinea given by Government, and half-a-guinea to the brother or relation in the regiment who is the cause of bringing him up ; and if the recruit chooses shall only be attested to serve during the present war with France, by which time probably the term of both their services will nearly expire together."

On the 80th of March the following appeared in the orders of that day :--"As the evening parades of the regiment will be the resort of the military and the ladies to *admire the Tyrone Boys*, the Lieut.-Colonel expects the men will come remarkably clean as well as in the morning—the hair to be well powdered, neat, and well done, and the shoes well blacked."

Family money being at this time paid to those women who had remained at home, an order was issued on the 17th of April to officers commanding companies to send in a correct list of the married men whose wives had never left the county, in order to have the certificates filled up. " They will mention the time the husband marched from the county, the number of children under ten years of age, and if a volunteer or ballotted man, and if the latter, for what parish. These certificates to be sent to the men's wives, who will get them signed by two magistrates, and the family money will then be paid, on producing the certificate at the Treasurer of the County's Offices, Omagh, from the day the husband left the county." It appears from a subsequent order to the foregoing one that there was a second class at that time entitled to family money or allowances from the county. The order was this :—" Unmarried men, whose fathers or mothers, from age or infirmity, were rendered unable to get their bread and depended on them for support, or whose fathers and mothers being dead, and their brothers or sisters being under the age of 10 years and depending on them for their support, those persons being then actually residing in the county, were to get certificates for which, when signed by two magistrates and presented to the Treasurer, they would then receive payment." On the 28th of April the Marquis's and Captain Dobbin's companies were ordered to Carrick-on-Shannon, and the Major's and Light Infantry to Boyle until further orders. The gunners of these companies marched with them to their stations. The remaining six companies were ordered to hold themselves in readiness to march on the shortest notice, either the whole together or in detachments. On the 15th of May the regiment was to prepare to take the field on the shortest notice, and for this purpose tents for the officers were provided by the Government, but a stoppage for the price of them was to be made from the usual allowances of bat, baggage, and forage money. On this order being issued, Lieut.-Colonel Moore recommended to such officers as were not already provided with camp beds that they would supply themselves forthwith, or take advantage of being in a seaport to get made by sailors a cot to sleep in inside their tents.

The 4th of June being the anniversary of his Majesty's birthday, six companies at headquarters, with their field pieces, assembled at Fort Hill and fired—the former three volleys, the latter twenty-one rounds in honour of the day. The front of the Shamble Barrack was illuminated, and a barrel of beer was placed at the door of each company's barrack that the men might drink the King's health, and treat their friends of the town ; and as it was a general day of rejoicing, and trusting to the men's good conduct and behaviour, every liberty was given to them.

On the 6th of June, the first division of the Northampton

Fencibles arrived in Galway, after a long march and voyage, when Colonel Moore expressed a hope " that the men of the Royal Tyrone Regiment would treat them as brothers, and being strangers in the kingdom, they would give them every assistance in their power."

The six companies remaining in Galway up to the 12th of June were now ordered to the following stations, viz :—Captain Crawford's to Ballina, Captain Bailie's to Newport, Captain John Richardson's to Westport, Captain Stewart's to Claremorris, the Grenadiers to Elphin and Strokestown, and the Lieut.-Colonel's company to Ballinamore, in the County Leitrim. Each of these companies proceeded from Galway at three o'clock in the mornings of the 13th, 14th, 15th, 16th, 17th, and 18th of June. Westport being the head quarters of the regiment, the band was ordered there.

CHAPTER II.

THE first intimation I find of the removal of the regiment from these quarters to Dublin is by an order of the 9th November, 1795, " a Captain of the Royal Tyrone Regiment" for " the Castle Guard." The regiment at this time occupied quarters in the following barracks, namely :— the Palantine Square, Abbey Street, and Custom House. On the 21st of November, detachments were ordered to Rathcool, Swords, and Dunboyne, to be stationed there for one month. These detachments were relieved on the 19th of December. The following extract of a letter received by Lieut.-Colonel Moore from the Marquis of Abercorn, was communicated to the officers of the Royal Tyrone Regiment on the 19th of January, 1796 :—

" I must beg you, while the regiment is at Dublin, to be particulary attentive to the strict correctness and uniformity of the dress in our officers. They are not so well aware as I am how much regiments are distinguished by the minute observance of regimental propriety in every point of their appearance. They must always wear white breeches, with regimental boots, and never any other waistcoat than the uniform. Their black stock must be always close and tight about their necks, and no bow or tie in sight, and these particulars must be observed, not only on parade but off. While we are in Dublin, or camp, it will not be in your power to grant leave of absence. That our regiment is in all essential points excelled by none is doubtless owing in some degree to the residence of the officers, and while at Dublin, or near it, that residence is more than ever desirable. Afterwards I hope we may give every indulgence possible.

(Signed,)

ABERCORN."

Nothing worthy of notice then occurred with the Royal Tyrone Regiment from the date of the foregoing extract up to the 23rd of August, 1796, when Major General the Earl of Moira inspected the regiment, after which he directed Major Cole

Hamilton, who was then in command, " to return his thanks and express his highest approbation at the conduct of the regiment in the field that day." He also assured the major that he had not seen such steadiness before in any regiment, and that the exactness with which the different evolutions were performed demanded his warmest praise. On the 2nd of September, Lieut.-Colonel Moore, having joined from leave of absence, resumed the command of the regiment, which on the 12th of the same month was inspected by Major General Craig, who directed him to express his satisfaction to the officers and men of the regiment, and his approbation of their steadiness and exactness in their movements that day, notwithstanding the weather was so unfavourable.

On the 28th of October, the regiment was ordered to hold itself in readiness to proceed to its winter quarters in Kells, Coothill, Old Castle, and Trim, on the shortest notice. In consequence of this, six companies were ordered to march on Tuesday and Wednesday, the 1st and 2nd of November, as follows :—

| The Marquis's, Lieut.-Colonel Moore's Major Hamilton's, and Grenadiers, | Kells. | Captain Baillie's, Capt. C. Richardson's, | Old Castle. |

It does not appear when the remaining four companies, which were removed to the Custom House barracks after the above had marched, left Dublin for Cootehill and Trim, but that they occupied these quarters is evident from the fact that the monthly returns were forwarded from them to the headquarters at Kells on the last day of each month.

The enemy (the French) having dared to disturb the peace of this kingdom by attempting a landing in the south, the Royal Tyrone Regiment, on the 26th of December, 1796, was ordered to march forthwith to Cork. The following paragraph appears in connection with the orders of this removal :—" The commanding officer trusts that the men of the Royal Tyrone Regiment will show themselves on this occasion what they have always professed, and what they have been known for, steady and loyal."

It appears that on the line of march towards Cork, five companies were halted for some days in Nenagh, and five in the town of Roscrea, and subsequently, on the 2nd of February, the regiment was to march to Limerick as its destined quarters, instead of Cork, except the flank companies which where to be detached to form separate battalions. "Lieut.-Colonel Moore hoped the regiment would consider it as a particular favour shown to its discipline and good behaviour to be thus brought forward to the advanced part of the army, that it might not have to encounter the same fatiguing march it had before whenever the enemy may attempt a second mad invasion of this kingdom." On the 31st of January, 1797, the following extract from a general order issued from the Adjutant General's office, Dublin, was circulated among the troops in this kingdom :— " His Excellency the Lord Lieutenant has desired the commander-in-chief to convey his thanks to the generals, officers, and soldiers who marched with so much alacrity towards the enemy. The spirit of the troops, and the loyal exertion of every description of His Majesty's faithful subjects, warranted a well grounded hope that the enemy would have repented of his rashness had he ventured to land. But at a time when so much praise is due to the troops, the commander-in-chief feels it his duty to point out to them the necessity of the most active attention of every individual to the separate duties of his station, the attendance of officers with their regiments, a regular attention to their men, and the proper subordination of ranks in their various duties. For even the bravery of the soldier, unless amenable to orders, and on every occasion under control, is more likely to turn to his own disadvantage than the public good."

On the 19th of February, 1797, the Royal Tyrone Regiment was ordered to be augmented forthwith to 1,000 men ; therefore recruiting parties of officers, sergeants, corporals, and drummers were to be sent out immediately to the County Tyrone, for the purpose of raising the number of men required to complete the establishment. The men were to be enlisted for " during the war, and two months after, and to receive three guineas bounty, and the marching guinea then allowed." The light infantry companies of the Tyrone and Louth Regiments marched from Limerick to Kilkenny, on Monday the 27th of February. On the 4th of May the regiment was ordered to hold itself in readiness to march from Limerick to the following cantonments on the 10th and 11th of that month, viz :—three companies to Tarbert, three to Killarney, one to Dingle, one to Castleisland, and one to Tralee. This order was afterwards rescinded, so that the regiment was not then removed.

On the 6th of May, Major General Sir James Duff requested the commanding officers of regiments composing the Limerick garrison to acquaint the non-commissioned officers and men of their respective regiments, "that he had laid before the commander-in-chief their resolutions, expressing their sentiments of loyalty and determination to protect the Constitution of their country against all its enemies. Such principles cannot fail in securing them the love and gratitude of all loyal subjects, and their exemplary conduct while under his command entitled them to his warmest thanks and approbation."

On the 3rd of June, the Marquis of Abercorn, in order to mark the distinguished loyalty and the soldier-like conduct of the Royal Tyrone Regiment, and the meritorious example they so lately set to all other regiments, established a badge of merit in the regiment, to be worn by one hundred soldiers, selected from such men as had served full three years, in the proportion of ten to each company, two of whom only could be corporals.

The candidates for such mark of honour were to be men who had never been punished, (or who having been punished had redeemed their characters by a subsequent series of the most exemplary conduct), or confined in the black-hole, of good character, and not an officer's servant. The merit of the candidates to be determined by a board consisting of the four senior officers off duty and the adjutant.

Captains, or officers commanding companies, were to recommend to the board fifteen men of their respective companies, out of which number the board was to recommend to the Marquis ten of the most deserving; the remaining five candidates were to be the first on the list in the event of vacancies.

The order was to be distinguished by a silver medal, hung between the third and fourth button hole of the left lappel with a red ribbon, and with each medal a certificate on parchment, under the seal of the regiment, was to be delivered.

The Marquis also bestowed medals as honorary rewards to such sergeants as he judged most deserving, and supernumary ones were to be issued to such soldiers as would distinguish themselves. This badge was to be established on the 4th day of June, 1797, in honour of the birthday of the then Most Gracious Sovereign, King George the Third.

Having observed that the order of the 4th of May for the Tyrone Regiment to hold itself in readiness to move to the cantonments stated therein had been rescinded, on the 7th of June that order was renewed. Capt. C. Richardson's company marched to Dingle, and on the 13th, two companies, Captain Stewart's and the Grenadiers, marched to Killarney, and the Major's, Captain Baillie's, and Captain J. Richardson's to Tarbert. On the 22nd, Captain Burnside's company marched to Tralee, leaving two companies in Limerick, where they remained up to the 19th September, when the Lieut.-Colonel's company marched for Castleisland, and the Marquis's, with the gunners, for Tarbert.

As the regiment still occupied the foregoing quarters, nothing worthy of notice occurred, with this exception, that in the month of January previous, a soldier of the Tyrone Militia, while standing as a sentinel at Tralee, in the county of Kerry, was assassinated by a man disguised in woman's clothes—until the following letter was received :—

" Dated Dublin Castle, 3rd March, 1798.

Sir—Having taken the first opportunity of laying before the Lord Lieutenant, Major Arthur Cole Hamilton's letter of the 10th instant, addressed to the Marquis of Abercorn, communicating the unanimous resolution of the officers, non-commissioned officers, drummers, and privates of the Royal Tyrone Regiment of Militia, to subscribe the proportion of their pay therein stated towards the continuance and support of the present war, and adding, that if necessary they will continue the same during the war each year—I am commanded by His Excellency to signify to you his desire that you will communicate to the Royal Tyrone Regiment the high sense His Excellency entertains of this very signal and distinguished proof of its zeal and loyalty.

I have the honor to be, sir,

Your most obedient humble servant,

Lieut.-Colonel Moore, PELHAM."

Tyrone Militia, Tarbert.

On receipt of this letter the following regimental order was issued, dated 18th March, 1798 :—" Lieutenant-Colonel Moore has particular happiness in communicating to the officers, non-commissioned officers, drummers, and privates the foregoing letter he has received from the Right Honourable Mr. Pelham, in consequence of their very handsome resolution of contributing towards the present exigencies of the Government to repel the attack of a most inveterate enemy, should they persist in invading these kingdoms.

" As the several companies were unanimous in their loyalty, but differ only in their endeavours who should excel most in their gifts, the Lieutenant-Colonel has adopted what he has conceived the easiest and most effectual, that of the most moderate companies, namely—seven days' pay from the non-commissioned officers, drummers, and privates, and fourteen from the officers—half mounting allowance being an unequal

D

sum, in consequence of the augmentation, and would fall heavy on the old soldiers and very light on the recruit. Lieutenant-Colonel Moore will not fail to communicate the loyalty and general good conduct of the men to their colonel, the Marquis of Abercorn."

The alarm now seeming to increase, not only from foes without but from foes within the kingdom, a garrison order was issued on the 10th of April, 1798, to the following effect, that 3 captains, 6 subalterns, 6 sergeants, 6 corporals, and 150 privates "will march this night, on a particular duty, with their knapsacks and blankets." These men were to march in three divisions, each division to be joined by a detachment of yeomanry, the whole to parade at the appointed time in the barrack yard at Tarbert. These three divisions were under the command of Captain Vallancy, Captain J. Richardson, and Captain Johnston.

The particular duty that these detachments were to be employed on required the most perfect order to be at all times observed. "No party was to be detached without an officer, and the operation of each division was to be so regulated that they might mutually assist each other." One bugler accompanied each division on this duty.

As there was every reason at this time to suppose that in the change of quarters likely soon to take place, the Tyrone might be included, and as it was probable the regiment might be moved at a very short notice, every measure possible was to be taken so as to prevent any unnecessary delay; therefore, everything requisite for the men on the march was to be immediately provided.

The regiment was not kept long in suspense with regard to change of quarters, as it was ordered to march to Cork on the 18th of May following, leaving one company at Tarbert, until such time as the Sligo Militia, by whom it was relieved, should become acquainted with the exercise of the guns.

The following extracts are taken from Sir Richard Musgrave's History of the Irish Rebellion :—

"As the United Irishmen in the neighbourhood of Ballymore-eustace were known to have an immense quantity of arms, Captain Beevor was sent there on the 10th of May, 1798, with detachments of the 9th Dragoons, the Tyrone, Antrim, and Armagh Militias, to compel a surrender of them, by living at free quarters. He had every reason to believe that he had completely succeeded in the object of his mission, as he received three thousand stand of arms of different descriptions, and,

particularly, as on the morning of the 23rd of May four sergeants
of United Irishmen marched in their quota of men, eleven each,
with their pikes on their shoulders, and received protections.
This induced him to send off one hundred and twenty men of
his garrison, and keep about forty to lighten the distress of
the people who were obliged to maintain them.

"About the hour of one o'clock, on the morning of the 24th
of May, he was awakened by the cry of a person that the rebels
would have his blood ; and on rising, two men rushed into his
bed-chamber, one armed with a pistol the other with a pike.
The former, who fired at him, very fortunately missed him, on
which he seized a pistol, which lay at his bed-side, and shot
him through the body. The other made a lunge at him with
his pike, which he strove to avoid and received but a slight
wound in the shoulder. At that moment Lieutenant Patrickson
arrived, and ran the captain's assailant through the body.

" In the mean time the rebels set fire to several houses in
which the soldiers were quartered, and, assisted by the owners
who secreted their arms, murdered seven dragoons and four of
the Tyrone Militia, and desperately wounded three of the former
and two of the latter.

. " At length Captain Beevor sallied out with twelve dragoons,
and routed them in every direction. Lieutenant M'Farland, of
the Tyrone Militia, a most excellent officer, was shot through
the body and died.

"Lieutenant Eadie, of the Tyrone Militia, who had been
stationed for some months at Ballytore, was ordered on the
morning of the 24th of May to join his company at Calverstown.
Having proceeded with twenty-three privates by Narraghmore,
he received a pressing invitation there to breakfast, which was
very unfortunate, as by that delay he was prevented from
arriving in time to save the lives of the loyalists.

" He had not proceeded far with his party when he heard the
shouts of the savages, exulting over their victims as they conveyed them for execution.

"Lieutenant Eadie placed his men behind a low wall, and when
the savages came within thirty yards gave them a volley which
killed many of them.

" The rebels, after their defeat by Lieutenant Eadie, retreated
to Ballytore, when they gained a reinforcement of many thou-
sands, and learning from their scouts that he (Lieut. Eadie)
had missed the road to Calverstown, they pursued him.

" General Campbell having received intelligence that the
rebels were in great force in Ballytore, when he entered it he

found it deserted by every male except Mr. Francis Johnston, a surgeon; and as some of the Tyrone Regiment had repeatedly seen him commanding the rebels, the sight of him kindled such indignation in them that one of them bayonetted him through the breast, on which he fell, but rising again and with many oaths asserting his innocence, five of the Suffolk Fencibles shot him.

"On the 9th of June the Tyrone light companies were engaged in the battle of Arklow."

I regret exceedingly that so little mention is made of the Tyrone Militia in any history of the Irish rebellion which I have seen, as from my childhood I have often listened to the most thrilling narratives, told by the men of the light companies who had served through the rebellion, and who had witnessed the death of many of their comrades in the several engagements they had been in, and amongst the rest at Gorey and Vinegar-Hill.

One of those men was a Sergeant John Reilly, who was discharged on pension in 1815, and who only died a few years ago at Newtownstewart, in the County of Tyrone; another was Sergeant Robert Blair, who died while on the staff in Caledon, and whom I have often heard sing a song, the concluding lines of one verse being

> " Dundas cried out with all his might
> Tyrone Boys take the field."

A third was a Sergeant Pat. Walls, who was discharged on pension from the staff in Caledon, and a fourth was Sergeant John Mullen, who also died in Caledon after receiving a pension. I could name many others who belonged to the Tyrone light companies and who served through the rebellion.

The following circular was received from the Adjutant General's office :—

"Dublin, 11th June, 1798.

"The very rapid succession of gallant actions, which have almost daily been reported to Lieutenant-General Lake, has prevented his doing the justice to the army under his command which his feelings have prompted, by offering to them the public thanks due to their services. He most gratefully offers those thanks to the several generals, officers, and privates who have so highly distinguished themselves by their valour and good conduct in the trying engagements at Naas, Kilcullen, Hacketstown, Taragh-hill, Kildare, Rathangan, Mount-Kennedy, Carlow, Newtownbarry. Ross, Antrim, Arklow, and also in the many smaller actions which have taken place, as well as those he has enumerated.

" The gentlemen of the Yeomanry Corps have also acted in a manner so exemplary that General Lake cannot but consider the safety of the kingdom in the present struggle to have been essentially supported by their courage, loyalty, and indefatigable exertions.

" G. HEWITT, Adjutant-General."

In reference to the latter clause of the foregoing circular, I think it not out of place to introduce in this record the opinion of another general officer with regard to the loyalty of the yeomen in four of the counties of the province of Ulster, which I transcribe from Sir Richard Musgrave's History of the Irish Rebellion. It is as follows :—

" In the counties of Fermanagh, Tyrone, Derry, and Armagh there were fourteen thousand yeomen, and most of them Orangemen ; and they were so loyal and so well disciplined that General Knox, who commanded at Dungannon, reported in the summer of 1798, that he would rest the safety of these counties on their fidelity and bravery ; and much to the honour of the Presbyterians three-fourths of them were of that order.

" In Tyrone there were about five thousand yeomen, the majority of whom were Presbyterians, and there were about four thousand two hundred Orangemen among them."

At eight o'clock in the evening of the 5th of October, 1798, the garrison at Cork, of which the Royal Tyrone Militia was one of the regiments, fired a *feu de joie* in honour of the glorious victory obtained by the British Fleet, under the command of Admiral Lord Nelson, over the French Fleet in the Mediterranean.

The Marquis of Abercorn having commanded the Royal Tyrone Regiment of Militia from its embodiment up to the month of November, 1798, now resigned, when Lord Viscount Corry was appointed colonel commandant, and was expected to arrive in Cork on the 13th November to succeed the Marquis, and his lordship having arrived as expected, all reports were ordered to be made to him.

The regiments at this time stationed in Cork were the following, namely—Berwick Dragoons, 41st Foot, 60th Foot, Tyrone Militia, Westmeath, Galway, and Meath Militias—General Officer of Brigade, Major General Myers.

Cork, 1st December, 1798.—" Whenever the regiment is ordered to march with light baggage, the men are only to carry the following articles, namely—a pair of shoes, soles and heels, two shirts and a comb, in a small bag that will be provided, which is to be rolled up in their blankets. The knapsacks to be left behind under the care of a careful non-commissioned officer, and will always be brought forward to the men when in a settled situation. The sixty rounds of ammunition to be carried in pouches and magazines; with this and three or four days provisions the men will find themselves much loaded, but not too much to prevent their marching with rapidity if necessary. It is also recommended to the officers to provide themselves in some similar manner, as in case of an active campaign in this country they will often be reduced to the blankets for a covering, and the haversacks for provisions."

16th December.—I find a memorandum for the sergeant-major—it is as follows:—" The sergeants at all times to appear with clean leather gloves, and leather sword knots on the swords; when off duty to carry sticks in their hands. The corporals doing lance sergeants' duties to wear their epaulettes as corporals, and the lance corporals to have two bars of lace edged with blue across the right arm; those bars will be issued by Lieutenant Anderson."

It appears there was a want of uniformity in the swords worn by the officers of the Tyrone Regiment at this time, and therefore Lord Corry expressed a wish that the officers in future should have the regulation swords, and as they were to be had in Cork, he would be glad they could be provided as soon as possible. There was to be no distinction in the swords worn by the field officers, staff, or flank company officers from those of the battalion.

4th January, 1799.—" After the officers have examined the arms, dress, and appointments of their companies every morning, they will put their companies through the manual exercise, prime and loading motions, and fire several times. The officer who exercises the company, as well as the supernumeraries in the rere, will be particularly careful that the motions are performed with attention and care, that the men are steady and upright under arms, and send all those who are not to the daily drill."

Memorandum.—7th January, 1799.—" The bags for the men's light baggage to be delivered to the companies to-morrow, and on Thursday next the regiment will appear in marching order with them instead of the knapsacks. They are to be folded in the blankets which are not to be increased in the length by them. The blankets are only to be used on guard for the men to sleep in, and not to be used as a covering while on sentry or patrole;

in these cases they are to be folded and strapped up. The non-commissioned officers on guard are to be responsible that this is attended to.

" Fevers increasing amongst the men, the sergeants are directed to attend to the cleaning of the barracks and fumigating the rooms and galleries with gunpowder, which will be delivered from the stores for that purpose."

From the concluding part of this memorandum, the anxiety of Lord Corry for the preservation of the health of the men of the Royal Tyrone Regiment is most apparent, and is worthy of all praise, as it manifests the regard he had for those under his command, that they might not suffer through a want of attention to cleanliness in their barrack rooms.

The following letter, dated Adjutant General's office, Dublin, 14th January, 1799, appeared in garrison orders at Cork on the 18th January in that year. It is as follows :—

" Sir—In consequence of repeated representations made unto Lord Cornwallis respecting the duties of the troops, His Excellency desires you will make such arrangements and issue such positive orders as shall prevent the soldiers in the forces under your command being at any time called on to perform any that can leave him less than two nights in bed, the present state of quiet in this country rendering it unnecessary that they should be exposed to greater fatigue."

Nothing worthy of notice having occurred in the orders of the regiment from the 18th of January, the following appeared in the garrison orders of the 10th February, 1799 :—

" Notwithstanding all the orders given for the cleanliness and regularity of the barracks, the quartermaster-general at his inspection found great fault. As the health of the men depends so much on this essential point, the officers who visit the barracks and the officers of companies must be more minute in their inspection, and when they have occasion to find fault they will not quit the barracks until the non-commissioned officers have them repaired. The beds are to be constantly folded up in the manner shown by the quartermaster-general, and the coals are to be put in the coal-boxes and not thrown on the floor. The boilers are never to be used for any other purpose than boiling the victuals, and the sergeants are to be responsible that the barrack women attend particularly to this. All the small temporary fire-places are ordered to be taken down. The officers and sergeants must set their shoulders to work to have the barracks in complete order, as they will be frequently visited by the quartermaster-general. The quartermaster-sergeant to go through the barracks once each day, and report anything contrary to these orders. Agreeable to the standing orders of the regiment, no sergeant's or corporal's wife can be employed as mess-woman or cook in the barracks. Officers commanding companies will immediately discharge such as may be thus employed, and employ the wives of the privates. The Roman Catholic clergymen have signified that the soldiers of their religion may eat meat four days in each week during Lent, the messes to lay in meat accordingly."

My reason for introducing the foregoing order into the record of the Tyrone Militia is to show the care and anxious concern of the authorities for the health of the troops under their command, at this crisis of our country's history when the spirit of rebellion was not yet fully subdued, and as it appears from the following circular from the adjutant-general's office, Dublin, 21st February, 1799, that our (then) enemy, the French, was still exciting and fomenting this spirit of rebellion in the hearts and minds of the disaffected Irish, such precautions were undoubtedly necessary to keep the troops in that state of health which would enable them on a short notice to take the field. Circular alluded to—"Sir—It being now certain that the enemy is rising every exertion to fit out another and more formidable armament destined to act against this country, I am directed by His Excellency the Marquis Cornwallis, to refer you to the standing orders of the 12th of April, 1797, etc., to desire you will take the necessary measures for ascertaining whether the several regiments under your command be complete in every article requisite for march against an enemy, and for procuring a supply of their respective deficiencies, should any such at this late period exist, etc. The Lord Lieutenant desires you will point out to the commanding officers of regiments the indispensable necessity of the utmost precision on the subject, and their responsibility for the complete equipment of their men for the field. I am further directed by His Excellency to desire that you will order all officers now absent, not recruiting, or under very strong circumstances, to be immediately called to their regiments, and that you will not forward any further memorial for leave of absence, except in such very extraordinary cases as you may judge necessary to attend to.

" I have the honor to be etc., etc., etc.,

"G. HEWITT, A.G."

Major General Myers.

In consequence of this general order to be in readiness to

take the field against the expected enemy, the following regimental arrangements were to take place and to be duly attended to.

The present men called Pioneers were to be henceforth called Camp Colour Men, and to march each with a camp colour, and to carry their arms and accoutrements on march, and to be formed in one section in the rere under their present sergeant and corporal, while the following men were to be called Pioneers, and were to march at the head of the regiment, having in charge the car, with the intrenching tools, hatchets and saws; they were to wear the Pioneers' caps and aprons on all parades and on march, and whose business was to open gaps and remove obstacles out of the way of the column :—

Corporal Robinson, Henry M'Elhanna, Grenadiers; Oliver Kelly, Captain John Richardson's; Edward Slevin, Major's; Pat. Murray, Colonel's; William M'Cristall, Capt. Johnston's; Michael Loy, Captain Burnside's; Andrew Carson, Captain M'Causland's; Michael Mallon, Captain Charles Richardson's; and Walter M'Fadden, Lieut.-Colonel's company.

In the month of March, 1799, Captain Baillie had received a letter from Lord Corry, in which his lordship expressed a wish, at the same time accompanying that wish with an order, that the officers should complete themselves immediately with the new sword, and one of the new coats with the pattern buttons, so that in case of an immediate inspection or review the whole might be uniform, as by the middle of April his lordship expected that the very old coats of the officers would be worn out, and such as were not were to be altered to the new shape, having the new pattern buttons, so that by the 20th of April there should not be a second sort of regimentals.

In connexion with this order, I find that on the 11th of April the commanding officers of regiments were to remind the officers that the day was approaching in which they were to appear in their new uniform and swords, and as they had such long notice it was expected none of the old uniforms nor swords would be seen on parade or in the streets, as there might yet be an inspection before the 20th of April, and if so they must appear in their new appointments.

The French still threatening to join the Irish rebels in this kingdom, an order from the Assistant Adjutant-General's office, Cork, dated 12th April, 1799, was promulgated to the general officers commanding brigades, in which it was stated that " in the event of an enemy landing in this kingdom, they were strictly enjoined to prevent any women from accompanying the

E

army on its march, that they were to be left behind in charge of the officer who remained with the heavy baggage of the regiment, and who was to pay them 4d. per day for their support, and 6d. per week for lodging. This order Lieutenant-General Lake called the particular attention of the general officers of brigades to, and to enforce the due execution of it in the strongest manner."

By a general order dated Cork, 6th of May, 1799, the several regiments in the southern district were to hold themselves in readiness to march at a moment's warning, agreeable to Lieut-General Lake's orders of the 30th of September, 1798, and in consequence of this order the men of the Royal Tyrone Regiment were forthwith to be completed to sixty rounds of ball cartridge and two flints each per man ; they were also to have the bags with their light baggage rolled in their blankets, so as to be ready on a moment's notice to march.

Major General Myers having signified his intention to Lord Corry that he would inspect the Royal Tyrone Regiment on Monday the 13th of May, and that his inspection would be very minute with respect to the clothing and arms of the regiment, " his lordship therefore expects that the general will have no occasion to find fault with the appearance of the men at the review, that their coats will be mended, and their breeches and leggings good. The officers to appear in boots, with sword-knots on their swords, gorgets with purple rosettes, and clean buff leather gloves, and in future the gorgets to be worn by the officers on guard."

After this review, Major General Myers requested Lord Corry to express his approbation to the officers and men of the Tyrone Regiment for their steady and soldier-like appearance in the field on this occasion.

Lieutenant-Colonel Moore having resigned on the 30th of April in this year, Lord Corry was pleased to appoint Major the Honourable A. C. Hamilton, Lieutenant-Colonel, and the Hon. Du Pré Alexander to be Major—both commissions dated 11th June, 1799.

It having been represented to Lord Corry that several men of the Tyrone Regiment had behaved in a very unsoldier-like manner, attended with a great degree of impertinence, at the public office, respecting the National Bank Notes which had been issued as subsistence by an order of Government instead of the Bank Notes of the town of Cork, which were not negotiable except under particular circumstances, and that the soldiers of no other regiment had behaved in this manner, Lord Corry therefore directed that the officers commanding and paying companies would take every possible means to explain to their men " that should they have any dispute relative to the passing of National Notes for things purchased by them, that they bring the person who refuses to the office of Mr. Courtney, who would explain the matter to the satisfaction of both parties."

Lord Corry hoped " that the men on such occasions would show every civility and good manners, and not by foolish and impertinent behaviour, such as Corporal Shaw exhibited that day, bring disgrace on the regiment, as a little perseverance would bring the National Bank Notes into full circulation, and be the means of producing plenty of gold and silver."

On the 30th of June I find the following regimental order issued :—

" The regiment to parade to-morrow in marching order, the long roll and bugle to sound at seven o'clock. The officers to appear with their haversacks and canteens, and the men without powder, the hair well combed and neatly clubbed and very smooth. A review of necessaries will take place when the regiment returns, in order that such men as have not their marching necessaries in their bags may be punished. At the morning inspection the officers are to examine the cap cases, as many of the men have made a practice of stuffing their cases with rags, and putting their caps in their knapsacks. The commanding officer of the regiment most strictly forbids any ribbon, flower, or mark of distinction of any club or society in the regiment whatever being worn to-morrow, except the order of merit of the regiment. He will be much concerned if he finds himself placed under the necessity of punishing or finding fault with any of the regiment for disobedience of this order."

Towards the latter end of the month of July in this year, the Lord Lieutenant was expected to visit the garrison at Cork, and there was every reason to suppose he would inspect the troops in garrison ; Lord Corry therefore requested " that the officers would be particularly attentive to see that the men's coats were properly mended, and that every man had a good pair of breeches, and their arms in proper order, as the officers could not pay too great attention to those points at their daily inspection. And with respect to the officers themselves, his lordship not only hoped but expected the greatest uniformity would be observed in their dress, agreeable to the orders of the regiment, that their hats would be worn with the proper part in front and over the right eye, and that no part of the hinder

cocks would be brought to the front ; they were also to wear
roses on the hair, to have regimental swords and sword knots,
which latter was to be worn constantly from that day, and to
have uniform long boots."

It being notified that His Excellency the Lord Lieutenant
would arrive in Cork about the hour of eleven o'clock on the
3rd of August, a guard, consisting of 1 sergeant, 1 corporal,
and 12 privates, was ordered to mount immediately on his
arrival. On the following day he inspected the troops in
garrison, and on the 5th of August " Major General Myers was
commanded to communicate to them His Excellency's entire
satisfaction with the soldier-like and good appearance of the
men in the field ; and in addition he, Major General Myers,
begged them to accept his thanks for their steadiness."

In connexion with His Excellency's and Major General
Myers' expression of approbation to the troops in garrison,
Lord Corry also had the satisfaction of informing the Tyrone
Regiment that their particular steadiness had not passed un-
observed by him that day, and in consequence of which, he
directed that all prisoners, with the exception of a man named
James Doran, be released from their confinement, " trusting
that the praise their comrades had that day received would
stimulate them to good behaviour, so that they would not
subject themselves to such constant confinement, which in
the end becomes disgraceful to a soldier." Lord Corry adds
" the officers of the regiment are most particularly entitled to
my best thanks, for their great attention to the general principles of manœvures and exercise as ordered by the general
officer, and for the very particular manner in which they
marched past and saluted His Excellency."

On the 12th of August, 1799, the following general order was
issued from the Adjutant General's office, Cork :—

Tyrone Militia, Caithnes Legion Fencibles, Notting-ham Fencibles, Devon and Cornwall Fencibles, Louth Militia. " Lieut.-General Lake desires you will order the regiments men-tioned in the margin to hold themselves in readiness to march at a moment's notice, agreeable to the printed regulations of the 12th of April, 1797.

" Should there be any difficulty in procuring cars to carry
the baggage of the regiments, the general desires you will please
to order them to be immediately pressed, but if they can be
procured whenever they may be required, there is no necessity
for getting them until the regiments are ordered actually to march.

Major General Myers.   " N. MASSEY, A. General."

In consequence of the foregoing general order, the following morning regimental order was issued.

"The Tyrone Regiment being one of those ordered by the Marquis Cornwallis to march in the event of the appearance of the enemy on the coast of this kingdom, it is the commanding officer's orders that the regiment holds itself in such a state of readiness as to move on the shortest notice. The regiment to parade until further orders, morning and evening in marching order, and to take only their light baggage and camp equipage. The officers are most particularly requested to take nothing but a very small portmanteau with their blankets, for which purpose a few cars will be appointed.

"When the regiment pitches its tents for a night or two, only one private tent will be allowed for the officers of one company, and in case of a longer stay on the same ground the marquees will be put up if necessary. Lieutenant Boirreau, Sergeant Samuel Hanley, and Sergeant M'Crossan to remain in Cork with the heavy baggage and women ; particular orders will be given for his conduct.

"Surgeon's-mate Burkitt to remain with the sick, and Surgeon Sinclair will move with the regiment; a car will be appointed for his medicine chest. All officers' servants, while the regiment remains in its present state of readiness, to be properly dressed as soldiers, so that they may be ready to fall into the ranks on the first alarm. No excuse whatever will be allowed for any servant being left behind on any business of his master's. The officers will do right to send as soon as possible their heavy baggage, or such as they may not want, to the regimental store. All officers off duty to attend the morning parades, and one officer of each company in the afternoon, when constant inspections, morning and evening, are to take place of the men's necessaries ; and too much care cannot be paid to the articles of shoes, soles and heels. Each company will find the advantage in the event of a long march to have a few pair to take with them. Such ammunition as may be damaged in the men's pouches to be changed immediately for good, and each man will be supplied with a good flint from store on application to Sergeant Bragg. The marksmen of each company, and all the sergeants, to have powder in their hair, which will be issued on application to Sergeant Bragg. Sergeant Mercer, with the camp colour men, to form the constant baggage guard, which will be increased as circumstances may require each day, but the whole will always be commanded by an officer. The men to cook two days' provisions to-morrow, so that they may have one day's cold to carry in their haver-sacks."

14th August, 1799.—"When the regiment marches on the supposition to meet the enemy, no women is on any account to accompany it; should any be found disobeying this order, she will be punished with the utmost severity. Agreeable to the orders of Government each woman is to receive fourpence per day, and sixpence per week lodging money, during the absence of her husband; twopence per day of which is to be paid by the soldier, and will become a charge against him. The officer left in charge of the baggage will have the payment and arrangement of this, as well as the subsistence of the sick men. His first care will be to put all the women and children out of the barracks, and the sick to be collected into rooms as convenient as possible. The remainder of the barracks to be delivered to the barrack-master, taking his receipt for them and the furniture. The convalescents and men not able to march to be placed as guards on the several barracks until delivered up; and if the officer and sergeant left behind are attentive and active to this part of their duty, there will be no charge for loss of furniture, which would fall heavily on the married people. Whenever the regiment is ordered to march, the convalescents and men that are to remain behind will assemble in the rere of the regiment, with their arms under the command of the officer and sergeant appointed to command them, when he will receive further directions."

Cork, 23rd August.—"The men of the Tyrone Regiment in the Bridge Barrack to remove to-morrow to Jamieson's Barrack, which has been completely washed, cleaned and put in repair—the former barrack being condemned—and in order to preserve the cleanliness and health of the latter, the men are to eat their dinner and breakfast in the large cooking shed, which is also to be kept clean. No tables to be admitted into the barrack rooms. All washing and smoothing to be done in the shedding. Women transgressing this order to be turned out of the barracks. The yard to be kept very clean, where there are two pumps, one for common uses, and of which the water is not to be drank by the men, the other is the water from the pipes, and comes in every second day. Barrels will be prepared for the purpose of being filled. The officers who visit the barracks are to see this order carried out."

4th September.—"In consequence of the order for completing the light company forthwith, each battalion company will furnish two men for that service. They must not be under five feet seven inches, and twelve months in the regiment, well made and active. Volunteers from each company to be preferred. They are to be inspected by Lord Corry on the morning parade to-morrow in order to be shown to General Myers, and, if approved of, their accounts to be made up to the 14th instant inclusive, on which day they will be transferred from their present companies, and to be marched by a commissioned officer and sergeant, so as to arrive at Athlone on the 14th. A copy of the men's accounts to be signed by the commanding officer and given with their subsistence to the sergeant, who is to account for the same with the captain of the light company."

8th September.—The troops composing the garrison were ordered to be under arms at seven o'clock in the evening of the 9th, to fire a *feu-de-joie* for the great success of His Majesty's arms, under the command of Sir Ralph Abercrombie, K.B.

16th September.—"The regiment being now complete with cues, the officers in examining their companies at morning and evening parades, were to give the greatest attention possible to the manner in which the men dressed their hair, and to punish every neglect. The men were to be as well powdered at every evening parade as at the morning. The officers are to take particular care that their cues were not too far from the head, and that the whole are tied at the same distance, and that the cues are at all times well polished."

The following garrison orders appeared on the 18th Sept. :—
"The irregular conduct of officers in quitting their guards until regularly relieved, causes Major General Myers in the most positive manner to order that no officer quits his guard on any pretence whatever without orders, either day or night. The officers must dine at their guard rooms, examine all reliefs before they march off, and take the most decided means for every person under their orders doing their duty correctly and with activity ; and it having been represented to Major General Myers that the men are permitted to go home to their dinners from their guards, it is his most positive orders that such unmilitary practices are not to be allowed in future, and the officers commanding guards are to call the rolls every half-hour, and not permit a man to be absent on any account. Should any men of the guard be taken sick, they are immediately to be replaced by a man from the same regiment."

The annexed circulars from Dublin Castle, and from the Adjutant-General's office, Dublin, of the 9th and 12th of November, 1799, were addressed to Lieut.-General Lake, of the

Southern District at Cork, to make known to the troops under his command.

" Sir—The failing of the corn harvest rendering it peculiarly important to preserve the potato crop from injury, Lord Cornwallis desires you will direct the commanding officers of the corps in your district to permit the soldiers under their command to give such assistance in digging the potatoes in the neighbourhood of their respective quarters, as may be afforded without material prejudice to the service.

"I have the honor to be, etc.,

"E. B. LITTLEHALES."

" I am directed by His Excellency the Lord Lieutenant to desire that you will give immediate orders to the troops under your command to discontinue the use of powder or flour, until further orders, the late general bad harvest having rendered this measure indispensable.

" I have etc., etc.,

" G. NUGENT, A.-General."

Cork, 15th Nov., 1799.—Lieut.-Colonel Hamilton being now in command, directs that " every regulation of parade and dress ordered by Lord Corry be most strictly attended to, as he is determined to punish those who neglect it, as he is responsible to his lordship to deliver the regiment on his return in the same good order it was in at his departure. The attention and early attendance of all officers at morning and evening parades is now more necessary than ever, in consequence of the soldiers not wearing powder. The officers are directed to pay great attention to the dress of the men's hair without powder—that it is well greased and smooth, the side locks let grow longer and well put back with the grease, and the cues to be closer to the head than with the powder."

Cork, 20th Nov., 1799.—" In case of any alarm in the garrison, the drums of the main guard to beat to arms through the principal streets, and those of each regiment through their respective quarters. The guards will immediately double their sentries, and the remainder of the guard stand to their arms.

" The several regiments will assemble at their respective alarm posts, and there wait for further orders. As soon as they are assembled, each regiment to send an officer to headquarters, viz :—the Artillery in their own barrack yard to man the light six-pounders, the horses of which are to be harnessed but not taken out of their stables ; the Berwick Cavalry on the Grand Parade ; the Tyrone Regiment at the lower end of Patrick Street ; the Antrim Regiment in the Old Barrack yard ;

and the Carlow Regiment on the Terrace or South Parade."

Nothing beyond the mere routine of the daily parades and guard-mounting having occurred in the interim, I now come in my research to the close of the year 1799, and find a reference to what would be expected from the men of the Royal Tyrone Regiment by Lieut.-Colonel Hamilton, expressed as follows :—" The approaching holidays, it is hoped, will be passed over by the men of the regiment with the same order and good behaviour which has always marked their conduct on such occasions. To-morrow being Christmas Day, the whole of the regiment will attend divine service at their places of worship. The men's dinner will not be until three o'clock, when the officers of each company will attend at their respective barracks to see that the men sit down comfortably to it, and give such orders as they may think necessary for their enjoying themselves with propriety in their barrack rooms. There will be no evening parade, but the rolls to be called before the men go to dinner in the barracks." On the 26th of January, 1800, the following brigade order was issued at Cork, which appears to have been the first in reference to volunteering from the Irish Militia to serve in regiments of the line, the British army being then engaged in war with France. It was as follows :—

" Major-General Myers cannot for a moment doubt that the regiments of Irish Militia will not be actuated by the same principles and spirit that have so eminently distinguished their brethren in England, and that they will not as readily step forward and testify their loyalty at this moment that promises so much honour to the troops intended for general service, and which must eventually render so essential service to their country. Commanding officers will assemble their regiments by companies, read and explain most fully to them the general orders, and use their utmost to encourage their men to partake of their share in a contest wherein the honour, virtue, and courage of Great Britain have been so eminently displayed, and promises so glorious a finish to the war.

" It is ordered that where more than the number required turn out as volunteers that a draft be made by lot for those to go.

" To prevent any kind of irregularity, the soldiers are directed, after having determined on the regiments they wish to serve in, to report the same to the sergeant-majors of their regiments, who will keep a roll of their names and selected regiments, and as soon as a reasonable number have turned out they will be inspected, their accounts settled, their bounty

F

paid, and they will as soon as possible be sent to the regiments they have made choice of. Government has determined on the bounty, the orders will be explained to them, and nothing remains but their naming the regiments they wish to serve in.

"Major-General Myers makes no doubt that the reports he shall have to make of the regiments under his command will fully justify the idea he has hitherto entertained of their ardent desires for actual service. In the meantime, the utmost regularity and discipline will be expected, and he hopes on this occasion to experience the same order and good conduct which have hitherto distinguished the troops under his command."

When this order was made known to the Royal Tyrone Militia, who up to this time remained in Cork as its head quarters, the result was, that on the 31st January, 1800, no less a number than 227 men volunteered their services to regiments of the line from the nine companies then present as follows, viz.:—

From the Colonel's company, 16 men; Lieutenant Colonel's, 31; Major's, 31; Captain J. Richardson's, 38; Captain Charles Richardson's, 27; Captain Burnside's, 17; Captain Johnston's, 13; Captain M'Causland's, 34; and Captain Bailie's, (the Grenadiers,) 20—total, 227.

These volunteers all joined the 1st Royals, with the exception of one man named Hughes, who selected the 35th Regiment as his choice, and two named Reid and M'Crystall, who joined the 62nd.

The Tyrone Regiment, having been quartered in Cork from the latter end of July, 1798, up to the beginning of February, 1800, was now ordered to Trim and Kells, in the County Meath, four companies to the former, and six to the latter station, being headquarters of the regiment. In the months of February and March the volunteering to the line continued, when 176 men extended their services in the following proportions from the ten companies:—

From the Colonel's company, 12 men; Captain Bailie's, 7; Captain Sinclair's, 56; Captain J. Richardson's, 14; the Major's, 14; Captain Burnside's, 21; Captain Johnston's, 14; the Lieut.-Colonel's, 8; Captain C. Richardson's, 23; Captain M'Causland's, 7—total, 176.

Of these 176 volunteers, 126 joined the 1st Royals, 13 went to the 4th Regiment, 3 to the 35th, 1 to the 49th, 20 to the 54th, 2 to the 62nd, 10 to the 68th, and 1 to the 69th Regiment.

The regiment having given so many volunteers to the 1st Royals, the following officers of the Royal Tyrone were promoted to that regiment, their commissions bearing date the 17th March, 1800, namely—Lieutenant William Richardson, Lieutenant Thomas Campbell, Lieutenant George Carrothers, Lieutenant John Eadie, Lieutenant Skeffington Torrens, Ensign Richard Richardson, Ensign Charles Johnston, Ensign John Baxter.

Perhaps I should observe, in reference to the number of volunteers given by Captain Sinclair's company in February and March, that the men had not had an opportunity of extending their services while the headquarters remained at Cork, particularly as the regiment was then about to move to its new quarters in Trim and Kells. The regiment in a short time after its occupation of these quarters had three companies removed to Navan, one to Kilcock and Nineteen-mile-house, and a portion of one company to Ballinasloe, leaving at Kells, the headquarters, the Colonel's and Captain John Richardson's companies, and the remainder of Captain Charles Richardson's which was not sent to Ballinasloe; but in the middle of April this (the light company) was removed to Athlone from Ballinasloe, taking the portion of it which had remained at Kells to that outpost.

On the 5th of April I find that six other men of the Tyrone Regiment had volunteered to the 1st Royals, making the total number to that regiment alone 356 men.

22nd May, 1800.—The present state of the country in which the regiment was then unavoidably dispersed required the greatest attention possible to be paid by the commanding officers at outposts, to prevent the soldiers mixing with the inhabitants; for which purpose no man of the regiment was to be allowed to work for any of them without orders, either from the Lord Lieutenant or the general officer commanding the district. The commanding officer of the regiment particularly directed, in order to prevent this, that morning and evening parades should be regularly attended.

From the scarcity and dearness of provisions, which appear to have prevailed in the month of July this year, especially towards its close, and the consequent distress which many of the married men and their families had to suffer, the commanding officer permitted the married soldiers to assist the inhabitants in making up their hay in harvest, but in no other work, and the sergeants of the companies had to give a return of the men so employed at every morning parade, and as the men came from work every evening they were to show themselves to their sergeants, who, if they found any of them under the influence of liquor, were to confine them. The names of the persons, and place in which they lived, for whom the men worked were to be given to the sergeants.

Brigadier General Barnett having signified his intention on the 7th of September that he would inspect the regiment on the 18th of that month, the detachments at Navan and Trim, as well as the smaller ones at Ratoath, Dunshaughlin, and Garretstown, were to meet the headquarter detachment in the field at a place called the Six-mile-stone, on the road from Trim to Kells, and four miles from Navan, where the inspection was to take place. The entire regiment, except the light company stationed at Athlone, were assembled at this field for exercise on the 15th, 16th, and 17th September, and on the 18th General Barnett inspected the regiment there according to appointment; and the commanding officer on the 19th said " he was very happy in having it in his power to notify to the officers, non-commissioned officers, and privates, the very high opinion Brigadier-General Barnett entertained of them for their very steady and soldier-like appearance in the field yesterday."

CHAPTER III.

THE Regiment having been now in Kells, Trim and Navan from the beginning of March up till the end of October, was ordered to Dublin to do duty there, for which station the first division of the regiment proceeded from Trim, joined by the detachments from Ardbraccan and Ratoath, on the 3rd of November, 1800, and on its arrival was to occupy the barracks in the Old Custom House, Dublin.

The detachment at Garretstown marched to Navan, which, with the two companies stationed there, proceeded to Dunshaughlin, and joined by the detachment at that place marched on Tuesday, the 4th, for the city; but this division and the headquarter's division from Kells, the latter marching by Trim, having to arrive at Dublin on the same day, were to meet and march in one division from the Black Bull, so that whichever division arrived at this point first was to wait the arrival of the other before it proceeded on its march. This latter division was quartered in the Royal and Rotunda Barracks.

Before the headquarters left Kells, Brigadier-General Barnett had the following communication addressed to Viscount Corry, or officer commanding Royal Tyrone Regiment, Kells, and dated the 1st November, 1800 :—

" Brigadier-General Barnett cannot allow the Royal Tyrone Regiment of Militia to leave his district without expressing to the officers, non-commissioned officers, and soldiers, his very high sense of their exemplary good conduct during a period of seven months that they have been in his district, and he has to regret that the service should have required their being called from under his command.

" Signed,

" J. LEE, Brigade Major."

The regiment being now settled in Dublin, with the exception of the light company which remained at Athlone, attached to the 2nd battalion of light infantry at that station, the strictest order that could be well conceived was issued to the regiment, not only with regard to the dress and appearance of both officers and men on parade and in the streets of the city, but in respect to the cleanliness and regularity to be observed in the men's barrack rooms, as Brigadier-General Dunne intended to inspect them as soon as possible, which he did, and as the health of the men was considered to be a matter of the first importance, the orderly officer visiting the barracks was directed by the commanding officer to be most particular in this duty, and if he had occasion to find fault he was not to leave until he saw that the rooms were perfectly clean.

The Dublin garrison duty at this time was, as it appears, rather severe on the troops, for not only had the different guards to be furnished, but also outposts both north and south of the city, and, moreover, as the brigade had frequently to appear in marching order, same as if the different regiments were about to move to other quarters, they had to form in the following order on parade—the Advance Guard, Camp Colour Men, Pioneers, Column, Baggage Guard with baggage on cars, camp equipage, etc., Rear Guard.

As the light infantry was still at Athlone, the advance guard was to consist of the sergeants and rank and file that remained in the regiment of those marksmen who had been selected in Cork, and under the command of Lieutenant Richardson.

This advance guard or company was subsequently increased to two subaltern officers, two sergeants, one bugler, and fifty rank and file. The second officer was Lieutenant Young.

As the union of England and Ireland took place on the 1st of January, 1801, the new union colours of the Royal Tyrone were marched down to the castle guard on that morning at half-past nine o'clock, under an escort of the entire grenadier company, with their officers in full dress, and with their bearskin caps.

In reference to this union of Great Britain and Ireland, the following circular was issued from Dublin Castle, 23rd December, 1800 :—

" Sir—On the 1st day of January, 1801, you will cause to be hoisted and displayed in the forts and fortresses within your district the new flags and banners established by His Excellency the Lord Lieutenant's proclamation in council, bearing date the 16th instant, wherein it is ordered and directed that on the union of Great Britain and Ireland certain alterations shall be made in the royal ensigns, armorial flags and banners, and His Excellency's commands having on the 18th of this month been issued to the quartermaster-general, and principal officers of the ordnance, to prepare the same conformably to the alterations required, it is presumed that they are now, or will be in perfect readiness at the time prescribed.

" When these standards or flags are hoisted as herein ordered, you will direct a royal salute to be fired by the guns of the fort or fortress where they may be so displayed, but it is not necessary that any other ceremony should be performed.

" I have the honor, etc., etc., etc.,
E. B. LITTLEHALES."

Lieutenant-General Craig, etc.

A brilliant victory having been obtained by His Majesty's Fleet, under Admirals Sir Hyde Parker and Lord Nelson, before Copenhagen, His Excellency the Commander-in-Chief ordered that a royal salute and a *feu-de-joie* should be fired by the troops in Dublin garrison on the 20th of April, 1801, and in consequence of this order the whole of the infantry off duty was to parade in the Royal Barracks on that day at twelve o'clock, and march from thence to the quays, the left of the line to be at Essex Bridge and the right towards the Queen's Bridge—each man to be provided with three rounds of blank cartridge. One squadron of the 24th Light Dragoons to be on each flank of the line of infantry; the brigade of artillery at Island Bridge was to fire a royal salute at the same time in the Phœnix Park.

Another glorious victory having been gained by His Majesty's forces under the command of General Sir Ralph Abercrombie over the French in Egypt, another *feu-de-joie* was fired by the troops in Dublin garrison on the evening of the 5th of May, they occupying the same position along the quays as on the former occasion—from Essex Bridge to the Queen's Bridge, and flanked as before by the 24th Light Dragoons, and the brigade of artillery firing a royal salute in the Park at the same time.

On the 9th of May Lord Corry appointed the Hon. Major Du Pré Alexander to be Second Lieut.-Colonel, without a company, in the Tyrone Regiment.

The following is the copy of a private letter addressed to Lord Viscount Corry, dated Dublin Castle, 30th July, 1801 :—

" My Lord—It appearing probable that an invasion of England may be attempted at no great distance of time, it is his Excellency the Lord Lieutenant's wish, upon communication with the commander of the forces General Sir William Meadows, to be informed whether your lordship thinks that, in case of such an event, your regiment would be disposed to volunteer its services into England for the immediate defence of that part of the United Kingdom.

" It is His Excellency's further wish to hear your lordship's answer immediately, and according to the result of it you may expect to hear again on the subject.

"Although it is by no means advisable that the matter should be given out in general order, nevertheless, His Excellency and the commander of the forces have no objection to your making such use of this communication as may enable your lordship to ascertain the sentiments of your regiment, and to report the same to me.

" I have the honour to be, etc., etc.,
" CHARLES ABBOTT"

Lord Viscount Corry, etc.

I regret that I cannot trace out Lord Corry's reply to the foregoing letter, which would appear from the following communication on the subject to have given much satisfaction to the Lord Lieutenant :—

" Dublin Castle, 4th August, 1801.

" Sir—Having laid before the Lord Lieutenant your letter of the 1st instant, containing the offer of the Tyrone Regiment of Militia to extend its services to any part of the United Kingdom, I have it in command from His Excellency to express the satisfaction he has derived from this additional proof of the zeal and loyalty of your corps, and his firm persuasion that should the emergencies of the country require the aid of this branch of the Irish Army, that it will be actuated by the same spirit and attachment to His Majesty's person and Government, which has at all times manifested itself in the Militia of Ireland.

" His Excellency has further authorised me to assure you that in the event of your regiment being so employed, a suitable and proper provision will be established for the wives and children of those soldiers who had, on this occasion, so handsomely volunteered their services, and that the best means of effecting this just and liberal gratuity on the part of His Majesty's Government is under immediate consideration.

" I have etc., etc., etc.,
"CHARLES ABBOTT."

Lieutenant-Colonel Hamilton, etc.

The surrender of Alexandria on the 2nd of September 1801, to His Majesty's arms, having been announced to the commander of the forces, he ordered a *feu-de-joie* to be fired on the occasion by the army under his command, which was carried out in the same manner along the quays, as those were when the former victories were achieved under Admirals Sir Hyde Parker and Lord Nelson over the French fleet, and by Sir Ralph Abercrombie over the French army in Egypt, the line extending from Essex Bridge to the Queen's Bridge, and flanked by a squadron of the 24th Light Dragoons.

The following letter accompanied this notification :—

"Adjutant-General's office, 26th Oct., 1801.

"General Sir William Meadows is proud to notice the impression made upon the troops under his command by the first and signal successes of the army in Egypt. The enthusiastic spirit which pervaded the whole army, and the offers generally made of unlimited service will be remembered as honourable to the troops and as worthy of the British character.

"The career of victory which has terminated in the entire conquest of Egypt, and complete overthrow of every remaining part of a numerous and veteran French Army, can alone be attributed to a continuance of the same heroic spirit, and strict observance of discipline, which has already been pointed at as an example to all who desire military fame or fall for the honour or welfare of their country. As such, the commander of the forces is confident the lesson will not be lost, and he looks forward to every officer and soldier being animated by a view of such events, to a persevering exertion towards the maintenance of good order and discipline, so that when the occasion shall again occur, their conduct may be stimulated by past actions, and may uphold the preeminence of the British arms."

"P. TYTTLER, A.-A. General."

A garrison order, to the following effect, was issued on the 3rd of November, 1801, that two captains, four subalterns, eight sergeants, four drummers, and two hundred rank and file from each of the regiments in the garrison of Dublin, were to parade on the 4th of November in the Royal Square, at half-past one o'clock, under the command of the field officer of the day, and that each man was to be provided with three rounds of blank cartridge, which they fired when marched to College Green, and "formed round the statue of King William the Third of glorious memory."

The officers of the Royal Tyrone Militia detailed for this duty were Captain Johnston, Captain Eccles, Lieutenant Sanderson, Lieutenant Brien, Lieutenant Osborne, and Ensign Hyde.

On the following day, the 5th of November, a firing party consisting of one captain, two subalterns, two sergeants, two

G

drummers, and one hundred rank and file of the Royal Tyrone paraded in the Royal Square at ten o'clock, under the command of the field officer of the day, for the purpose of celebrating that day according to usage. The officers present of the Tyrone Regiment were Captain Johnston, Lieutenant Young, and Lieutenant Edwards.

The parole on the 4th was "King William," and on the 5th "Discovery," both being very significant in their meaning as to the object for which those firing parties were ordered by the authorities at that time in command of the troops in Dublin.

The Tyrone Regiment, with the exception of the light company which was still retained in Athlone, attached to the 2nd battalion of light infantry, having been quartered in Dublin from early in the month of November, 1800, was now, in consequence of the termination of the French war by the surrender of Alexandria, ordered to return to the County Tyrone, for which it marched from Dublin in three divisions —the first on the 17th, the second on the 18th, and the third on the 19th of February, 1802, which were stationed in the county as follows :—1st Division : Captain Burnside's, Captain James Richardson's, and Captain Johnston's companies marched for Aughnacloy, under the command of Major Sinclair. 2nd Division and Staff of the Regiment : the Grenadiers, the Colonel's, and Captain M·Causland's companies marched for Omagh, under the command of Lieut.-Colonel Lord Alexander. 3rd Division : Captain Eccles', Lieut.-Colonel's, and Major's companies marched under the command of Major Richardson, and were quartered as follows, viz. :—Captain Charles Eccles' company, Newtownstewart; the Lieutenant-Colonel's company, Aughnacloy ; and the Major's company, Omagh. The light company, on its joining the regiment from Athlone, was also sent to Newtownstewart to be stationed there.

" Omagh, 16th March, 1802.

" To-morrow being Saint Patrick's day, the companies in honour thereof will parade in their new clothes, and as clean as possible, at 12 o'clock, and in commemoration of that day eight years when the regiment marched out of its county, the companies will have a field day and exercise as a military commemoration of the event, and to mark during that period the steadiness, loyalty, sobriety, and good conduct of the men who have discharged their duty as brave soldiers when called upon, without the empty praises of the populace of every town where they have been quartered, but meeting the highest applause from every general officer under whom they have served, and the warmest thanks of their officers belonging to the regiment, whose wishes and exertions would have availed nothing but for the good conduct of the men themselves."

By Express Circular—

"Royal Hospital, 2nd April, 1802.

"Sir—I am commanded by the commander of the forces to acquaint you that the definitive treaty of peace was signed at Amiens, at four o'clock in the afternoon of the 27th ultimo, by the plenipotentiaries of His Majesty, and the plenipotentiaries of France, Spain, and the Batavian Republic, on which happy event the troops under your command will fire a *feu-de-joie* as usual.

"I have the honour to be, etc.,

"F. BECKWITH."

Brigadier-General Hart, etc.

In compliance with the above order, the garrison of Omagh paraded in the Main-street on the 6th of April, to fire three volleys. The cavalry formed on the right and the yeomanry companies on the left of the Tyrone, they (the Tyrone) firing the first volley and after them the yeomen, and so alternately until the three volleys were fired, the band playing in the intervals, and the drums beating. Upon this occasion there was an illumination in the town of Omagh, to celebrate the victory of the British army over the French.

The definitive treaty of peace having been ratified, the disembodying of the militia was a measure that must soon follow, but, as the precise period was uncertain, it was thought highly necessary by the commanding officer that no more furloughs should be granted, but that all non-commissioned officers, drummers, and privates should remain at their quarters until the Government order for the final disembodying of the regiment should arrive. In the meantime the following general orders and circulars were received:—

"Adjutant-General's office, Dublin, 3rd May, 1802.

"General Orders.—The commander of the forces, General Sir William Meadows, has great pleasure in thanking the militia of Ireland for their good conduct in general since he has had the honour of being at their head. He is extremely pleased to find that they have marched into their own counties to be disembodied with regularity, sobriety, and good order, in proportion to the spirit which they marched out of them when the enemy was supposed to be meditating an invasion.

"For his own part he should ever be ready and proud to undertake the defence of Ireland at their head, assisted by the line and the yeomanry, against any force the enemy could bring against it.

"The commander of the forces cannot pass over in silence the very handsome and officer-like report he received from Brigadier-General Scott upon the breaking up of his fine corps. And he returns his thanks to Brigadier-General Scott, his officers, and the light infantry companies who have so creditably represented, and done such honour to their different regiments, and shall have great satisfaction in representing General Scott, and the officers he makes such honourable mention of to His Royal Highness the Duke of York, commander-in-chief.

"W. RAYMOND, D. A.-General."

Lieutenant-General Gardiner.

"Londonderry, 3rd May, 1802.

"Sir—I am directed by Brigadier-General Hart to apprise you of his intention of reviewing the regiment under your command on Thursday, the 13th instant, at Omagh, at which place you will assemble the several detachments from the regiment for that purpose. The principal object of this inspection is in order to pass the clothing, which the general requests you will have in readiness.

"I have the honour to be, etc., etc.,

"THOMAS WOOLDRIDGE, B.M."

Lieutenant-Colonel Hamilton,

Tyrone Militia, Omagh.

"Dublin Castle, 5th May, 1802.

"My Lord—Having directed a warrant and letter of instructions to be transmitted to you for disembodying the regiment of militia of which your lordship is colonel, the first and most gratifying part of the duty I have to discharge, is to communicate, in obedience to the king's command, to the officers, non-commissioned officers, and men through you, the high sense with which His Majesty is impressed of their uniformly good conduct since they have been embodied, and of their truly meritorious zeal and public spirit under all the trying occurrences which have arisen to call forth their loyal exertions during the long and arduous contest in which we have been engaged.

"It is particularly gratifying to me that from a return of peace having occurred during my administration, I am not only called upon to signify to your lordship His Majesty's gracious approbation of the meritorious services of the Tyrone Regiment of Militia, but that His Majesty should also be enabled by the fortunate event to which I have referred, to retire the corps from those arduous duties in which they have been so long and so honourably employed, and I cannot entertain a doubt that the loyal and patriotic spirit by which your lordship and the officers of your regiment have been actuated, will make a due impression upon the minds of the inhabitants of your county, and will continue to produce the most salutary effects in regard to its peace and tranquility.

     " I have the honour to be my lord, etc.,
Colonel the Earl of Belmore,   " HARDWICKE."
  Tyrone Regiment of Militia.

By the Lord Lieutenant General and General Governor of Ireland.
HARDWICKE,
    " Whereas the militia of the County Tyrone under your directions and command hath been embodied according to law for the safety and defence of that part of His Majesty's United Kingdom of Great Britain and Ireland called Ireland ; and whereas a definitive treaty of peace hath been agreed upon between the belligerent powers ; and whereas His Majesty is most desirous to take the first opportunity of relieving his faithful subjects from the burthens and expenses occasioned by the war, and has for that purpose signified to us his will and pleasure that the militia of Ireland should with all convenient speed be disembodied,
  " Now, We do therefore hereby order you, with all convenient speed, to cause the militia of the said County of Tyrone to be disembodied, and to issue all the necessary and proper directions on your part for returning the said militia under your orders to their respective parishes and places of abode. And for so doing this shall be your warrant.
  " Given at His Majesty's Castle of Dublin, the 5th day of May, 1802.
     " By His Excellency's command,
       " E. B. LITTLEHALES."
To the Earl of Belmore, Colonel of
  the Tyrone Regt. of Militia, or, in
  his absence, to Lt.-Col., or other
  officer commanding for the time
  being, of the said Tyrone Militia.
     " Dublin Castle, 13th May, 1802.
  " My Lord—The Lord Lieutenant having communicated with the commander of the forces upon the subject of the deposit of the arms and accoutrements of the militia corps in the event of their being disembodied, I have His Excellency's commands

to acquaint you that he is of opinion that the depôt of the arms and accoutrements of the Tyrone Regiment of Militia should be in a store in the town of Omagh, and desires that you will be pleased to provide a proper store at a reasonable rate accordingly, such store to be approved of by the general, or staff officer, under whose inspection the disbandment of the regiment will take place.

"It is expected that the county will make due provisions for the payment of the store for the deposit of the military arms.

"I have the honour to be, etc., etc.,

"E. B. LITTLEHALES."

Colonel the Earl of Belmore, or⎱
   officer commanding Tyrone ⎰
   Regiment of Militia, Omagh.

A store having been provided for the deposit of the arms and accoutrements, and the regiment inspected by Brigadier-General Hart, it was disembodied on the 13th of May, 1802; the staff then consisted of the adjutant, surgeon, 42 sergeants, 50 corporals, 20 drummers, and 2 fifers. In the number of sergeants the sergeant-major and quartermaster-sergeant were included.

By a general order, dated adjutant-general's office, 4th May, 1802, no accommodation in barracks or lodging money was to be allowed to the staff, and permanent non-commissioned officers of the militia upon their being disembodied.

This order, depriving the staff of barrack accommodation or lodging money, would appear to have pressed very hard on the officers, as well as the married men with families, whose pay at this time was not what it is now, did we not consider the vast difference in the price of provisions, which were then only about half what they are now, and have been for a lengthened period in the past. The pay of the adjutant then was 6s. per day; the surgeon's, 4s.; sergeant's, 1s. 6d.; corporal's, 1s. 2d.; and the drummer's, 1s. There does not appear to have been any distinction then between the pay of the sergeant-major, quartermaster-sergeant, and that of the sergeants.

The following is a list of the officers, taken from the muster roll of the regiment on the 24th December, 1801, and who were serving with it up till the disembodiment in May, 1802 :—

COLONEL—
The Earl of Belmore.

LIEUTENANT-COLONELS—
Honourable A. C. Hamilton.
Lord Viscount Alexander.

MAJORS—
George Sinclair.
John Richardson.

CAPTAINS—
George Vallancy, Adjutant.
M. J. Burnside.
John Johnston.
J. M'Causland.
Charles Eccles.
J. M. Richardson.
Charles Richardson.

LIEUTENANTS—
Richard R. Lodge.
James Speer.
William Walsh.
Alex. Anderson, Paymaster.
James Brien.
John W. Kyffin.
Samuel Armstrong.
Robert Saunderson.
James Taylor.

Thomas Young.
Matthew Edwards.
W. Fawcett.
Alexander Saunderson.
John Moore.
Charles Borrieau.
Robert Richardson.
Stewart Osborne.
Thomas Bailie.
John Creighton.
Ralph Macklin.

ENSIGNS—
Chas. Vallancy, Quartermaster
John Brien.
Alexander Boyle.
John Hyde.
Francis Graham.
John Crawford.

SURGEON—
William Hamilton.

ASSISTANT SURGEONS—
John Sinclair.
Francis Scott.
Walter Crofton.

CHAPLAIN—
Stewart Hamilton.

CHAPTER IV.

THE peace of Europe being again disturbed by another outbreak of war on the part of France, a circular letter, dated Dublin castle, 22nd December, 1802, was addressed to Colonel the Earl of Belmore, enclosing a printed copy of an Act passed in that session of Parliament, entitled an " Act for the more effectual enrolment of the Militia of Ireland, and for filling up vacancies therein." This intimation, no doubt, carried with it the conviction that the Irish Militia would not remain much longer in its disembodied state, which turned out true, for the following communication relative to the embodying of the Royal Tyrone Militia was forwarded to Lord Belmore, dated—

" Dublin Castle, 25th March, 1803.

" My Lord—The Lord Lieutenant having been pleased to order one company of the regiment of militia under your command to be drawn out and embodied, I am directed by His Excellency to signify to you his desire that you do proceed in the following manner, viz. :—

1 Captain, 1 Lieutenant, 1 Ensign, 4 Sergeants, 5 Corporals, 2 Drummers, 65 Privates. " The company is to consist of the number mentioned in the margin (the sergeants, corporals, and drummers to be of course taken from the present permanent embodied militia of the county,) and you will call upon the captain and subalterns of the said regiment, according to seniority, to attend at the place appointed for assembling the said company, it being intended to embody the militia in the proportion of one captain, one lieutenant, and one ensign to each company of sixty-five private men, and in proportion of one captain and two lieutenants to each flank company of regiments that are entitled to flank companies."

In this letter Lord Belmore was informed that instructions were sent to the Lords Commissioners of the Treasury for issuing pay to the company, and, also, as to the power he had in appointing an agent and paymaster to the regiment, and he was to issue the proper orders for arms and accoutrements to be delivered out of the regimental store for the company to be embodied, also in respect of providing clothing of the same pattern and quality as that supplied for regiments of the line, and that patterns of this clothing were to be laid before the board of general officers with all convenient speed for their inspection and approbation, so that measures would thereafter be taken for the payment of the clothing, to be provided as herein directed, of which his lordship would be duly informed. This letter concludes thus :—

"His Excellency further desires that you will issue the necessary orders for the immediate attendance of the surgeon belonging to the corps at the place appointed for the assembly of the company. Instructions will be sent for the government of his conduct as early as may be practicable.

"I have the honour to be, etc., etc.,
"E. B. LITTLEHALES."

Colonel the Earl of Belmore,
    Tyrone Militia.

"Dublin Castle, 21st March, 1803.

"Circular—My Lord—A resolution having passed the House of Commons authorizing the Lord Lieutenant to augment the bounty for recruiting the militia, I have His Excellency's command to acquaint you therewith, and to signify to you that you are to consider yourself authorized to augment the bounty in the following manner, viz. :—the sum of two guineas to be paid down to every recruit enrolled from the 25th instant, in the regiment of militia under your command ; every such recruit being drawn out, embodied, and assembled, one guinea more is to be laid out in necessaries for him, making the sum of three guineas, besides the marching guinea which each man is entitled to receive on his being marched out of the county to which he belongs, under the 97th clause of the 33rd of the king, chapter 22. Money from time to time will be issued for this service without delay, on your application for that purpose, and upon returns of the men so enrolled being transmitted to this office.

"I have the honour to be, my lord, etc., etc.,
"E. B. LITTLEHALES."

Colonel the Earl of Belmore,
    Tyrone Militia.

In pursuance of the order contained in His Excellency's letter of the 25th of March, the Earl of Belmore proceeded at

H

once to carry out its instructions with regard to the embodiment by companies of the Royal Tyrone Militia, according to the seniority of the captains and subalterns, and on the dates hereinafter specified, with the names of the officers, and dates of joining at embodiment :—

Companies.	Rank and Names.	When Joined.
Capt. Chas. Richardson's company embodied 31st March, 1803.	Capt. C. Richardson, Lt. R. Richardson, Ensign A. Boyle.	31st March, 1803
Major Sinclair's company embodied 4th April, 1803.	Major Sinclair, Lieutenant Lodge, Ensign Hyde.	4th April, 1803. 13th ,, ,, 11th ,, ,,
Capt. Burnside's company embodied 5th April, 1803.	Captain Burnside, Lieut. Armstrong, Ensign Bailie.	5th April, 1803. 8th ,, ,, 5th ,, ,,
Captain Eccles' company embodied 9th April, 1803.	Captain Eccles, Lieutenant Brien.	9th April, 1803. 18th ,, ,,
Capt. Jas. Richardson's company embodied 10th April, 1803.	Capt. J. Richardson, Lieut. Creighton.	10th April, 1803. 18th ,, ,,
Lieut.-Col. Hamilton's company embodied 17th April, 1803.	Lt.-Col. Hamilton, Lieut. Kyffin, Ensign Graham.	17th April, 1803. 14th ,, ,, 23rd ,, ,,
Captain M'Causland's company embodied 23rd April, 1803.	Lieutenant Borrieau	23rd April, 1803.

These seven companies, embodied on the above dates, were completed each in seventy rank and file, but the remaining three companies were not embodied until the month of May, when the colonel's and the two vacant companies were called up, and the establishment of the regiment in rank and file amounted to 690 men, wanting only ten to be complete. At this time, and for some time after, the company officers were greatly diminished by death as well as resignation.

On Wednesday, the 11th of May, the regiment was inspected at Omagh, by Brigadier-General Hart, at one o'clock, p.m., on that day, of which inspection due notice had been given by Brigadier-Major J. Coulson, of the Londonderry district, and on the day previous the regiment was medically inspected by Staff-Surgeon Comins.

On the 12th of May, Brigadier-General Hart was pleased to

communicate to the officer commanding the Tyrone Militia through the Brigade-Major, John Coulson, that the good disposition of the officers, and the satisfactory appearance of the men brought together at Omagh, so lately embodied at that place, "afforded him every hope of his being soon gratified by seeing the discipline of this regiment in such a state of forwardness as not to be exceeded by any other."

Some difficulty appears to have existed with regard to obtaining a suitable field at this time for the purpose of drilling the regiment at Omagh, which caused an amount of correspondence with the authorities at Dublin Castle, but which obstacle was ultimately removed by the hire of a field for exercise, at the annual rent of fifteen pounds, which was sanctioned by the Lord Lieutenant at the suggestion of Lieutenant-General Fox, then the commander of the forces in Ireland; but where this field was situated is not recorded.

" Quartermaster-General's Office,
" Dublin, 23rd June, 1803.

" Sir—I have the honor to acquaint you that your regiment will shortly be ordered to march from their present quarters to Limerick, and you will be pleased to hold them in readiness accordingly.

" I have the honour to be, etc., etc.,
" THOMAS BROWNRIGG."

Officer commanding Royal⎫
Tyrone Regiment, Omagh.⎭

The regiment having received the above notification that they might hourly expect a route, the men were apprised that it was impossible for passes to be given as long as this uncertainty existed; but should the commanding officer receive any information that the regiment was likely to remain at Omagh for any length of time, the indulgence of passes would be given as usual.

The following regimental order was issued, dated—

" Omagh, 29th June, 1803.

" The commanding officer of the regiment takes the earliest opportunity for informing the officers of the regiment that he knows not the moment an order may be received to march to a garrison town. He therefore desires that all officers who are not provided with the dress agreeable to the standing orders of the regiment, will forthwith equip themselves in every particular agreeable to the orders, with the exception of the feather, which is to be strictly conformable to the king's order, instead of the one entirely white, as heretofore worn by the regiment. It would be necessary for officers who are deficient in any appointment to make the greatest expedition in equipping themselves complete, as the commanding officer expects to find a strict uniformity to this order on the first parade after the arrival of the regiment at the quarters to which it may be ordered. The officers are likewise desired to allow no time to elapse in preparing their baggage, so that, on receipt of a route, the regiment may be enabled to move on the shortest notice."

It having been represented to the commanding officer in the beginning of July in this year, that the sergeants could not dress their hair according to Lord Belmore's order without the use of soap, and as the commanding officer was determined to carry out his lordship's order in every particular, he granted the sergeants the indulgence of using that article, and warned them at the same time that no excuse would be taken for their hair not being dressed according to the pattern shown on that day's parade.

"Dublin Castle, 16th July, 1803.

"Circular—My Lord—I am commanded by the Lord Lieutenant to acquaint you that from the 25th day of July, instant, inclusive, an effective captain will be placed upon the establishment for each of the companies now held by the lieut.-colonels and majors of the regiments of militia. You will therefore be pleased to nominate two gentlemen duly qualified for those companies for His Excellency's confirmation. The lieutenant-colonels and majors who, in consequence of this arrangement, are to cease holding companies, will continue to be paid as field-officers and captains, and allowed twenty pounds per annum each, in lieu of the non-effective dividend which captains of companies are entitled to receive. It is, however, to be understood that these field officers are to remain responsible for the accounts of their respective companies until effective captains are actually appointed, and have taken charge of those which were so held by them.

"I have the honour to be, etc., etc.,

"E. B. LITTLEHALES."

Colonel the Earl of Belmore,
    Tyrone Militia.

Notwithstanding the notification issued from the quarter-master-general's office on the 23rd of June, as to the movement of the Royal Tyrone Regiment from its quarters in Omagh to the garrison of Limerick, they remained still in the county up to the beginning of the month of August following ; the route being then received, a party, consisting of one subaltern, two sergeants, two corporals, one drummer, and thirty privates, was ordered to proceed at six o'clock on the morning of the 6th of August, to Dublin, there to receive the camp equipage for the regiment, which was to be escorted to the headquarters.

This party was to be chosen men of good character, and not married, and was to be subsisted for twenty days at 1s. 1d. per day.

Previous to the regiment leaving Omagh, Major Sinclair took the opportunity to remind the men of the former steady behaviour and good character the Tyrone Regiment ever bore on similar occasions, and he hoped it was unnecessary for him to make any further remarks, though he assured them at the same time that he was determined to punish every irregularity that would be committed by them until they arrived at quarters.

The following was the order of march, namely :—

First division, Sunday, the 7th of August, 1803, consisting of the following companies and officers :—1, the Grenadiers, Capt. James Richardson. 2, the Major's, Lieutenant Armstrong. 3, Captain Hamilton's, Lieutenant Kyffin. 4, the Colonel's, Ensign Boyle, Ensign Hyde.

Second division, Monday, the 8th August, 1803—1, Captain Eccles' company, Captain Eccles. 2, Lieutenant Colonel's, Lieutenant Taylor. 3, Captain M'Causland's, Lieutenant Speer, Lieutenant Saunderson, Ensign Crawford.

Third division, Thursday, the 18th of August, 1803—1, Captain James Richardson's company, Captain Burnside. 2, Captain Burnside's, Captain C. Richardson. 3, Light Company, Lieutenant Bailie, Lieutenant Creighton.

The first and second divisions having arrived at Limerick on the 20th of August, two companies were ordered to proceed on detachment to Bruff, Hospital, and Croom, on the 22nd, to relieve those of the 17th regiment who had been stationed there, the 17th regiment being removed from Limerick to Dublin.

The following officers were in charge of those detachments :— Bruff—Captain James Richardson and Lieutenant Lodge. Hospital—Captain Hamilton and Ensign Boyle. Croom—Lieutenant Speer.

It would appear from the precaution which it was now thought necessary to use, that the authorities at Dublin Castle were apprehensive that an incursion might still be attempted on the garrison at Limerick, and, therefore, stringent orders were issued that double sentries should be posted on the Irishtown side of Ball's Bridge, at seven o'clock at night, for the protection of large boats brought up from the Abbey River and moored at that point, which, it is to be presumed, belonged to the Government ; and that these sentries were not to be taken off until seven o'clock the following morning. Moreover, commanding officers of regiments were requested to make every necessary arrangement for the turning out of their men by night in the shortest possible time on any sudden call, and for this purpose it was suggested that the soldiers, when going to bed, should accustom themselves to place their clothes and arms so near them that they could lay their hands upon them in the dark. To ascertain that these necessary arrangements were made by the men, the officers of companies were directed to visit occasionally their barracks during the night, in case it should be found necessary to turn out in the night during that season ; if so, the men were not to delay to put on their gaiters, but to bring them to parade with them.

On the 80th of September, the light company of the Royal Tyrone Militia proceeded by route to Bandon, to join the light companies of the other regiments which were brigaded there.

Lieut.-General Tarleton having inspected the troops composing the garrison at Limerick on the 15th September, the commanding officer of the Royal Tyrone had it in command from him to notify to the regiment his high approbation of its soldier-like appearance, and in so doing he felt the most sincere pleasure, and thorough confidence that the regiment will ever sustain its long established character for correct and soldier-like conduct.

It would appear from the constant repetition in the orders issued from the brigade-major's office in the months of November and December in this year to the troops in Limerick garrison, that the Government authorities were then apprehensive of some invasion or sudden attack being made, as in almost every order some allusion was made to marching against the enemy ; anticipating such an event, the troops paraded with their camp equipage, intrenching tools, and necessaries on all marching order parades, and their heavy baggage was to be in readiness to be delivered into store on the shortest possible notice.

The regiment, having been quartered in Limerick from August, 1803, was removed to do duty in Dublin garrison in July, 1804, where it remained until the month of September, 1805, when it was ordered to Cashel, in the county of Tipperary, as headquarters, giving detachments to Tipperary, Thurles, and Cloonany, the light company occupying the latter station. The regiment remained in these quarters up to the end of July,

1806, when it removed to Clonmel, and in the beginning of the month of October following was ordered to Wexford, as head-quarters, giving a detachment of two companies to Duncannon Fort, and detachments to Enniscorthy and Newtownbarry ; and on the 30th July, 1807, a corporal and four privates were ordered to the signal post at Cahore point, near Gorey. In the year 1805, 133 men volunteered to the line; and in 1806, 146 extended their services.

On the 30th Sept., a garrison order was issued, in obedience to His Majesty's command, to say that he had permitted a proportion of the militia to enlist into the line, and had appointed the 36th, 43rd, 50th, 63rd, 69th, 73rd, and 81st regiments to receive volunteers from the Royal Tyrone Militia, and subsequently the 40th regiment also. The bounty then given to volunteers for unlimited service in the line, was fourteen guineas, and for seven years, ten guineas ; upon this occasion one hundred and ninety-two men of the Royal Tyrone volunteered their services into the line, the greater number of whom appear to have joined the 81st regiment, from the fact that Lieutenant William Hyde of the Tyrone was commissioned as ensign in that regiment, and marched these volunteers to Dundalk, which also appears to have been then its headquarters.

On the 1st of January, 1808, routes were received for the removal of the Royal Tyrone Militia to Dundalk in four divisions. The first division, consisting of the grenadiers, Captain Gorge's, and light company, with the staff and band, marched from Wexford on the 5th. The second division, consisting of Captain Moore's, Captain Armstrong's, and Captain Goodlatte's companies, marched on the 7th. The third division, Capt. Lodge's, and Captain Burnside's companies, marched on the 8th, and the fourth division, Captain Robert Richardson's and ·Captain Charles Richardson's companies, marched on the 9th of January, 1808.

Previous to the regiment leaving Wexford, the following brigade order was issued :—" Brigadier-General Peter cannot allow the Royal Tyrone Regiment of Militia to march from Wexford without expressing the highest approbation of the conduct of both officers and men while he has had the honor of commanding them. The attention paid to duty, and the exemplary conduct of the regiment, will merit the approbation of every officer they may serve under.

" By order,
" J. WALKER, B.-Major.

In the month of February, 1808, another opportunity presented itself to any man of the regiment who wished to volunteer into the line, but on this occasion only twenty-nine men extended their services, but into what regiments does not appear; while in the latter end of January and month of February no less than three hundred and twenty-three recruits were raised in the county, and joined the headquarters in Dundalk. These recruits were afterwards designated in the regiment as the "wet day boys," from the almost incessant rain which it appears attended them on their march.

The stay of the regiment in Dundalk was of very short duration, as on the 1st of March routes were received to remove to Kilbeggan, Moate, and Clara—Kilbeggan to be headquarters, in which Captain Charles Richardson's, Captain Goodlatte's, Captain Armstrong's, and Captain Burnside's companies were stationed. The grenadiers, Captain Moore's, Captain Robert Richardson's, and light company occupied quarters at Moate, and Captain Gorge's and Captain Lodge's companies, Clara.

The regiment moved to these stations on the 2nd, 3rd, and 4th of March, but its stay was even for a more limited period than at Dundalk, as it was moved again to occupy quarters in Limerick in the beginning of April, from which it sent out detachments to Patrick's Well, Croom, and Bruff, on the 13th of April; and on the 3rd of June, Captain Charles Richardson's company marched for Nenagh, to be stationed there.

On the 4th of June, the troops composing the garrison in Limerick fired a *feu-de-joie* in honour of His Majesty's birthday.

Another order for volunteering to the line having been issued from the brigadier-general's office on the 23rd of August, which order was to continue in force for three days in succession, seventy-one men of the Royal Tyrone in those three days volunteered their services to the regular army.

On the 17th of September nearly all the entire regiment was sent to different out-quarters from Limerick, as follows :—

Stations.	Majors.	Captains.	Subalterns	Sergeants.	Drummers	Rank and File.
Tarbert, ...	1	1	2	5	2	105
Askeaton, ...	...	1	2	5	2	105
Shanagolden, ...	...	...	1	2	1	35
Listowel,... ...	...	1	1	6	1	108
Hospital,... ...	...	...	1	2	1	46
Bruff, ...	...	1	1	4	1	78
Mount Catherine,	...	...	1	3	1	50
Patrick's Well,*...	...	...	...	...	...	5
Total, ...	1	4	9	27	9	532

* This was in addition to the first detachment.

In the month of October, eighteen men of the Tyrone
volunteered their services to regiments of the line, and five in
the month of May, 1809—two of the five to the 46th, two to the
69th, and one to the 90th regiments. In consequence of the
regiment having been scattered in different out-quarters on
detachment as above, almost from the time it arrived in
Limerick as its headquarters in April, 1808, nothing, save
the daily routine of garrison and regimental orders as to field-
days, parades, and officers for duty, or such like, occurred until
routes were received for the removal of the regiment for another,
and its last, tour of duty in the garrison of Dublin, while it then
remained embodied.

These routes were received on the 16th of June, 1809, and
the regiment marched in four divisions from Limerick—the first
on the 20th, second on the 21st, third on the 22nd, and the
fourth or last on the 23rd of that month, each division leaving
Limerick at five o'clock in the morning, and at the end of the
eighth day arrived in Dublin. The regiment at this time

occupied the barracks in Marlboro'-street, Old Custom House at Essex Bridge, and in Boot Lane.

It having occurred to me that the resignation of His Royal Highness the Duke of York, as commander-in-chief of the British army, is worthy to be recorded, I therefore insert a general order issued from the Horse Guards, dated 18th March, 1809, in the following terms :—

" Field Marshal His Royal Highness the Duke of York having requested His Majesty's permission to resign his situation on the staff as commander-in-chief of the army, and His Majesty having been graciously pleased to accept His Royal Highness' resignation, His Majesty has commanded it to be announced to the army that he has appointed General Sir David Dundas, K.B., to be commander-in-chief of his army, with the same authority with which His Royal Highness the Duke of York held that command.

" By His Majesty's command,
" HARRY CALVERT,
" Adjutant-General to the Forces."

In compliance with a circular letter addressed to the officer commanding the Royal Tyrone Militia, dated Dublin Castle, 2nd August, 1809, another volunteering to the line took place on the 8th of that month, when thirty-one men of the regiment extended their services to the following regiments : 8 to the 8th, 1 to the 48th, 1 to the 53rd, 2 to the 69th, 1 each to the 71st and 73rd, 8 to the 74th, and 7 each to the 82nd and 86th regiments, and in the month of November following twelve others volunteered, 1 to the 27th, 4 to the 71st, 3 to the 74th, and 4 to the 87th regiments.

Notwithstanding that recruiting parties were scattered throughout the County Tyrone, under the superintendence of officerrs of the regiment, and that many recruits were raised from time to time and sent forward to the headquarters, still the regiment was incomplete as it regarded its quota ; in consequence of this, in the years 1809 and 1810 frequent communications were received from Dublin Castle, by directions of the Lord Lieutenant, addressed to the officer commanding the Royal Tyrone, urging upon him the necessity of unwearied exertion to have the regiment completed one thousand rank and file, of which number it was generally one hundred and fifty men deficient throughout those years.

This, no doubt, was principally owing to the constant volunteering to the line which then prevailed, so that from the time of the augmentation the regiment does not appear to have been complete at any one period, nor did it seem possible to fill up the gaps unless resource was had to the system of balloting, the Act for which appears to have ceased on the 3rd of June, 1809.

Now I have to observe, that at the different periods of volunteering from February to November, in the year 1810, no less than one hundred and thirty two men of the Royal Tyrone extended their services to the following regiments of the line, namely—1st Royals, 2; 11th regiment, 10; 27th, 1; 44th, 1; 50th 6; 53rd, 1; 59th, 1; 61st, 1; 62nd, 7; 69th, 3; 71st, 3; 74th, 1; 75th, 19; 82nd, 3; 86th, 1; 87th, 5; 89th, 1; 90th, 1; 91st, 4; 100th, 31.

In 1809, on the 9th of December, Ensign Porter of the Tyrone was gazetted to the 86th, and on the 25th of August, 1810, Ensign Moorehead to 71st regiment.

The appointment of drum-major in the militia to the rank and pay of sergeant does not appear to have been sanctioned until the 25th of September, 1810, when a letter to that effect from the Lord Lieutenant was received from Dublin Castle by the officer commanding the Royal Tyrone Militia. Previously, the drum-major in the militia only ranked as drummer in his regiment; and it also appears by the same letter that trumpet-majors in the cavalry were raised at the same time from the rank of a trumpeter to the pay and rank of a sergeant.

The following communication, in reference to the band of the Royal Tyrone Militia, was received from the Assistant-General, dated—

" Dublin, 21st November, 1810.

" Sir—Referring to the answer transmitted by Major-General Coghlan to the observations of the commander of the forces on the extra number of the band of the Royal Tyrone Militia, I am directed by Lieutenant-General Sir Charles Asgill, in pursuance to orders received, to acquaint you that his lordship desires that the commanding officer of the regiment may be informed, that from the words of the Militia Act it does appear he may engage an additional number of drummers to be employed as musicians, but that the public are not in that case to be burthened with any part of the expenses of their pay whatever, and that therefore no deviation from the general order establishing the number of which regimental bands are to consist can he sanctioned by his lordship, unless it is proved that the expense of the extra musicians who may be so employed shall on no account become a charge to the public.

"I have the honour to be, etc., etc.,

"N. RAMSAY, Major A. A.-General."

Hitherto, I have made no allusion whatever to the band of the Royal Tyrone Militia, but the foregoing letter now induces me to say a little on the subject, as its character for its musicians was then second to none in the service. Under the instructions of its first-class bandmaster, Mr. Thomas Wilman, aided by his brothers Henry and John, this band had attained such a high degree of perfection as to attract notice and elicit the praise of the general public in all the quarters the regiment occupied, and, particularly the upper classes in society who could appreciate good music when well performed, and especially in the city of Dublin, where it was the favourite.

Its state dress, which I believe was ordered about this time by Lieutenant-Colonel William Stewart, then in command of the regiment, and which appears was supplied by a London house, and made after the pattern of that worn by the king's band, could not but be of the most magnificent and costly description, it being frequently asserted to my own knowledge that the pay of the (then) Earl of Caledon, as colonel of the regiment, during the years he was governor of the Cape of Good Hope, was absorbed almost, if not altogether, in paying for it ; therefore, I think it will not be considered out of place to give some idea, however imperfect, of the richness of this dress. In the first instance I will make allusion to that of the drum-major—he being the most conspicuous person from his position at the head of the band of the regiment, with whom I shall connect the band-master, both being dressed alike, with the exception of a shoulder belt which the drum-major wore, made of rich blue silk, embroidered partially with gold wire in rings, as a chain.

His cocked hat, and that of the band-master, was only distinguished from the other musicians by white feathers, the rest being red or scarlet, while all the hats were embroidered with heavy gold lace, deeply scolloped both in front and rere, rising from the cocks round the top.

The coatees of the drum-major and those of the entire band were embroidered with gold lace, but his and the bandmaster's were distinguished from the others by having suspended from both shoulders the same kind and description of ornaments then usually worn by general officers, called "Aiguillette."

The waist-belts of all were of the finest description of red Turkey leather, on which there were three rows of gold lace, interwoven in the centre with blue silk, and their sword-knots were also of gold lace, with good sized knobs at the end.

Their breeches were of the finest quality of white cassimere cloth, and they had white linen leggings with black patent leather straps, and plated buckles surrounding the leg under the knee.

The dress of the coloured, or black men, of which there were seven or eight then in the regiment, was still more magnificent. Their head dress was a turban of the most costly description. They had solid silver stocks and cuffs; their shell jackets were superfine scarlet cloth, same as the band, almost covered with gold lace and twist, which they wore over black cloth vests with sleeves. These vests had a gold lace stripe down the centre in front, and laced behind, the sleeves being embroidered from the elbow, to which the short sleeves of the shell reached down to meet the silver cuff.

The trousers were also of superfine scarlet cloth, with gold lace stripes down the side seams, and gold twist wrought in a fantastic form over the place of the pockets; and their boots were topped with yellow Turkey leather, which hung loosely round the small of the leg.

There were also two suits for the boys who beat the triangles on such days as the band wore the state dress. These were of the same description as those for the coloured men, with the exception of the head dress, stocks, and cuffs. The head dress for the boys was of scarlet cloth, with gold chain and tassel, and with a black woolly band about two or three inches deep round the bottom, and they were made almost as the busbies of the artillery are at the present day, excepting the piece of cloth which is connected with the latter on the crown, and which hangs over the side.

It was generally two of the smartest and handsomest boys, the sons of sergeants, who were selected on such occasion to act as trianglers, and for this honour there was generally a great number of competitors.

The regiment having been at this time on Dublin duty from the month of June, 1809, up to the month of April, 1811, was ordered to Galway, as headquarters, giving detachments to Oughterard, Loughrea, Woodford, and Eyrecourt.

On the 9th of July, 1811, a circular letter from Dublin Castle, was addressed to officer commanding the Royal Tyrone Militia, by command of the Lord Lieutenant, referring to an Act of Parliament then passed, permitting the interchange of the British and Irish militia regiments respectively, by volunteering to extend their services to all parts of the United Kingdom, and that His Royal Highness the Prince Regent, in the name and on the behalf of His Majesty, signified his pleasure that His Excellency the Lord Lieutenant should forthwith propose the extension of this service to the Royal Tyrone, and that the commanding officer would take the earliest opportunity of adopting the most effectual measures for carrying out the commands of His Royal Highness, by ascertaining what portion of the regiment was disposed to make the voluntary offer of extended service, so that they might be sworn in and enrolled for the militia of the United Kingdom in the manner prescribed by the Act.

It was fully explained both to officers and men the nature of the service in which it was proposed to them to engage, and this was that they could not be called upon for service out of Ireland for any longer period than two years successively, and that having once performed that period they could not under any circumstances, except those of actual invasion or rebellion, be again employed in Great Britain until the expiration of four years.

The officers who accepted this offer of extending their services were to be thenceforth placed upon the same footing in point of pay with officers of similar rank in the line.

The daily pay of the lieutenant-colonel up to this time appears to have been but 15s. 11d., now it was to be 17s. ; the major's, 14s. 1d., now 16s. ; and the captain's, 9s. 5d., now 10s. 6d. These are the only officers referred to specially in the circular, but it is to be presumed that the other officers of the regiment also obtained an increase of pay according to their rank.

The bounty granted by the Act of Parliament to non-commissioned officers, drummers, and privates on extending their services to Great Britain, was two guineas.

When this circular was promulgated, the entire regiment, with the exception of some six or eight men, extended their services ; but these subsequently volunteered also, as they did not like the epithet of "black belt," a name by which those were called who had, in the different militia regiments, refused to volunteer for England.

This Act, it appears, entitled both officers and men in the militia of the United Kingdom, if disabled in actual service, to all the advantages and honourable distinctions which had hitherto been confined to service in the regular army alone.

This circular further alluded to the readiness with which the regiments of militia had stood forward on all former occasions in support of the general interests of the country, and that this induced in His Royal Highness the confident belief that "their present extension of service would be as general as their sense of the advantages the empire would derive from this measure at that time, and that he could not doubt but they would feel the necessity of adopting the means then in their power for identifying the interests of Great Britain and Ireland, and that the confidence he thus reposed in the energy and patriotism of the militia would not be found to have been in any degree misplaced, but that they would most readily avail themselves of the opportunity of extending the field on which their services were henceforth to be displayed, and of rendering themselves to the United Kingdom what they had so long been to Ireland—a never failing-resource on every occasion of difficulty and danger."

At the several periods of volunteering to the line throughout the year 1811, fifty-two men of the Tyrone extended their services to the following regiments, namely :—to the 3rd, 6 ; 11th, 1 ; 18th, 2 ; 21st, 1 ; 27th, 1 ; 40th, 4 ; 42nd, 4 ; 56th, 4 ; 59th, 15 ; 66th, 1; 81st,1; 87th, 11 ; and 89th,1; the following officers were gazetted to regiments of the line at the following dates in the same year—Lieutenant George to the 75th foot, and Lieut. Abraham Taylor to the 82nd foot, both commissions dated 16th February ; Ensign Reynolds to the 89th, commission dated 2nd May ; and Ensign Cairnes to the 60th, commission dated 15th October, 1811.

An Act of Parliament having been passed at an early period of the session in 1812, to amend the laws relating to the Irish Militia, a communication, by command of the Lord Lieutenant, dated Dublin Castle, 29th of June in that year, was addressed to the colonel, or officer commanding the Royal Tyrone at Galway, to the effect that, as the regiment was incomplete in its establishment, it had been decided to bring into operation the provision of the first clause of that Act, by which one-fourth part of the whole number of persons to be raised in each year for the militia should consist of boys of the age of fourteen years and upwards. "The Lord Lieutenant therefore directed that the necessary measures would be adopted for enrolling such a number of boys as might be attached to the regiment under this authority, according to regulations. No boy was to be under five feet in height, with an appearance of growing, and was to undergo the same inspection as recruits raised for the militia, and to be attested according to the form of oath prescribed by the 2nd section of the Act of the 51st of the King (George III.), chap. 118.

" These boys were to be raised by beat of drum, same as other recruits, and to receive a bounty of four guineas, and a daily pay of 10d."

In compliance with this order, a number of boys were enrolled in this and the following year, among whom were a goodly number of the sons of men then serving in the regiment, and at headquarters with their fathers.

Sir James M. Stronge, Bart., who was appointed second lieutenant-colonel in the regiment at the augmentation on the 18th of February, 1806, resigned his commission on the 6th of April, 1812, in Galway; Major John Lindsay was promoted to be lieutenant-colonel in succession to Sir James; and Captain Acheson Moore, to be major, in succession to Major Lindsay.

The next move of the regiment was to Tuam, as its headquarters, where it marched in July, leaving its detachments in those out-stations they occupied from the time it arrived in Galway in April, 1811.

By an order from the adjutant-general's office, dated 24th August, 1812, a *feu-de-joie* was fired by the regiment to celebrate a glorious victory obtained by the allied army in the neighbourhood of Salamanca, under the command of General the Earl of Wellington.

In the year 1812 this regiment gave 93 volunteers to regiments of the line, as follows—Coldstream Guards, 3; the 6th foot, 1; the 8th, 5; 22nd, 12; 27th, 1; 29th, 21; 41st, 3; 50th, 2; 56th, 1; 67th, 1; 82nd, 1; 83rd, 5; 87th, 4; 90th, 1; 100th, 29; and 101st, 3.

Lieutenant Humphreys obtained a commission in the 100th regiment, to which he was gazetted on the 26th September, 1812; and Assistant Surgeon Alexander Sinclair was appointed to the 1st foot, on the 3rd of December, 1812.

In the month of April, 1813, in consequence of its being then intended by the authorities to remove the Tyrone Regiment to do duty in England, it was ordered from Tuam to Limerick, where it only remained until the beginning of May, when it proceeded to Cork, expecting to march direct to Cove (now Queenstown) for embarkation; but in this the regiment was disappointed, as after its arrival there a countermand was received, and it remained in Cork garrison until the beginning of February, 1814, when it was ordered to Clonmel.

In the year 1813, one hundred and thirty-two volunteers were given to the following regiments of the line—to the 8th, 2;

12th, 1 ; 16th, 4 ; 21st, 2 ; 22nd, 53 ; 32nd, 1 ; 37th, 3 ; 43rd 1 ; 70th, 38 ; 72nd, 9 ; 86th, 2 ; 88th, 7 ; 90th, 1 ; 97th, 3 ; and to the 100th, 5.

The following officers of the regiment obtained commissions in 1813 and 1814—Ensign John Caulfield, 22nd foot, in June, 1813 ; Ensign Gaston, 70th foot, in March, 1814 ; Lieutenant James Maxwell, 70th foot ; Lieutenant Arthur Stanley, 87th foot ; and Lieutenant Henderson Crozier, 22nd foot, on the 12th May, 1814.

I may here observe, that as the war had now virtually ceased no volunteering after the month of January, 1814, took place. In this month, one man volunteered to the 22nd ; and eight to the 70th regiment of foot.

On the 15th of April, the following communication was received :—

"Adjutant-General's office, Dublin, 14th April, 1814.

"General order.—Official intelligence having been received announcing the glorious and important events of the abdication of the Crowns of France and Italy, by Buonaparte, and the formal recall of Louis the Eighteenth, by the provisional Government of France to the throne of his ancestors, it is the commander of the force's orders, that a *feu-de-joie* shall be fired by all the troops and garrisons throughout Ireland, in celebration of these great and interesting occurrences.

"By order of the commander of the forces,

"J. HAY, A.-General."

I think it almost unnecessary to allude to the cheerfulness and spirit with which this order was acquiesced in and carried out by the Royal Tyrone, under the command of Lieutenant-Colonel Lindesay, as well as by the squadron of Dragoons, the Artillery, and Queen's County Militia, then in Clonmel, while the bands of the Royal Tyrone, and Queen's County regiments filled the air with their enlivening music of the "Downfall of Paris," both going to and returning from the field of exercise, and through the principal streets ; and the three hearty cheers which were given for the king, the British, and allied armies after the *feu-de-joie* was fired were most enthusiastic.

On the arrival of the regiment in Clonmel, a subaltern's detachment was stationed in Lismore, under the command of Lieutenant Bouchier, and continued to occupy those quarters, although the headquarters of the regiment was moved to Cashel in the month of July, 1814. At this time the greater part of the regiment was scattered on detachments in the following places in the County Tipperary, namely :—Cahir,

K

Tipperary, Callan, Ninemile-house, Ardfinnen, Ballyporeen, Littletown, Cappawhite, Mullinahone, Ardmoyle, New Inn, Mucklershill, and Kilmagenny. On these detachments, including Lismore, there were 2 captains, 8 lieutenants, 4 ensigns, 1 assistant-surgeon, 27 sergeants, 3 drummers, and 509 rank and file.

The regiment only remained in Cashel and its out-quarters for two months, when it was ordered to Tullamore as head-quarters, in the month of September, 1814. From this, detachments were sent to Longford, Mountrath, Granard, Borris-in-Ossory, and Donaghmore, and, in the month of October, other detachments were sent out from Tullamore to the following stations:—Lanesboro', Castletown, Horseleap, Clara, Ballynagar, Ballymore, Kilbeggan, and Moyvare.

As the result of the late abdication by Buonaparte of the crowns of France and Italy, and of his being exiled in the island of Elba, it was, no doubt, considered that the war with France was at an end, and that, therefore, arrangements might be adopted for disembodying the militia. With this view, a circular letter was addressed from the Adjutant-General's office, dated 10th June, 1814, to the general officers commanding districts, and through them to officers commanding regiments, as a preliminary step, " to give orders to all officers (except those attending Parliament), non-commissioned officers, drummers, and private men who were absent, to join their regiments immediately on their arriving in their respective counties, if their leaves of absence did not sooner expire, so that the necessary measures might be adopted, and the soldiers' accounts be in readiness for a final settlement upon receipt of the order for disembodying their corps. And so much importance was attached to the appointment of non-commissioned officers that colonels, or commanding officers, would see the propriety of using every circumspection in filling up such vacancies as might arise, more especially among the permanent class, as it was obvious that upon their steadiness and conduct depended in a great degree the future credit, appearance, and effective strength of the whole establishment."

In the autumn of 1814 a number of the Irish militia regiments returned to their respective counties and were dis-embodied; but the Royal Tyrone was not among this number, as it remained in Tullamore up till the month of February, 1815, when it received the route to march to Londonderry as its headquarters, leaving behind the detachments which were in Longford and Granard until the end of March following.

The state of the weather when the headquarter division left Tullamore was very severe, as the snow and sleet fell frequently during that long and wearisome march. The detachments from Longford and Granard were more fortunate in their move as fine weather accompanied them on their tiresome journey to Derry.

Shortly after the entire regiment had arrived at Derry, an order was received to discharge all men who had served five years and upwards.

This reduction was to be carried out at four periods, namely —on the 10th of May, 10th of June, 10th of July, and 10th of August, beginning with those who had served the longest on the 10th of May; at the same time any man who was fit to serve and who wished to remain in the regiment was re-enrolled for a term of five years, of which privilege many took advantage, and not a few were promoted to the rank of sergeants and corporals, to replace those who were discharged at that time, and recommended to the Board of Kilmainham for pension, which they obtained.

When the first period of reduction was over, a large flying party, as it was called, of the sergeants and corporals, with a good corps of fifers and drummers, under the command of Sergeant-Major Taylor, proceeded to the principal towns of the county to collect recruits, of which, on their first tour, they brought in a large number. One great attraction about this party was that the fifers and drummers employed on this occasion were bandsmen all dressed in the state clothing of the band, with a coloured man to beat the bass drum, also dressed in state clothing. This drew the attention of the populace towards the party much more than on an ordinary occasion, and, no doubt, was the cause of success.

Detachments of the regiment occupied quarters in the following places in the county of Donegal, during the time the headquarters remained in Derry, namely :—Buncrana, Carndonagh, Culdaff, Dunree-fort, Greencastle, and Malin, in which stations both officers and men were much harassed on revenue duty, though as a matter of course they were rewarded for each seizure they made.

The Derry Races having commenced on the 2nd August, 1815, such men of the regiment as were disposed to go to the race-course was to parade at a quarter before three, p.m., in the barrack yard, and to be marched from thence and back by the orderly officer of the day, agreeable to the garrison order.

The regiment being now reduced to the original standard or

quota from its augmentation during the war, the officers were also included in this reduction, therefore the services of the junior field officers, Lieutenant-Colonel John Lindesay, and Major the Honourable Henry Caulfeild, of the junior lieutenants of each company, and of the junior assistant-surgeon were dispensed with, and all the compensation the subalterns and assistant-surgeon received was two months' pay, and that without any claim to a retired allowance.

Immediately after the half-yearly inspection of the regiment on the 6th October, 1815, a brigade order was issued, from which I extract the following paragraph.—" The appearance and manœuvres performed by the Royal Tyrone Militia in the field this day was satisfactory to Major General Burnet, who is happy to observe that considerable attention has been paid to the improvement of the young soldiers, and advancement of the recruits."

On the 23rd of October, 1815, routes were received for the regiment to march for Birr on the 25th, 26th, and 27th of that month, when it proceeded according to the following arrangements :—

1st Division to march on 25th inst.	Captain Moore's, Captain Richardson's, Captain Armstrong's, and Capt. Brien's companies.	Commanded by Captain Brien.
2nd Division to march on the 26th instant.	Captain Lodge's, Captain Pringle's, and Capt. Miller's companies.	Commanded by Captain Lodge.
3rd Division to march on the 27th instant.	Grenadiers, Light Company, and Captain Boyle's.	Commanded by Major Irvine.

On the arrival of the regiment at Birr after another long and wearisome march, detachments were ordered to the following out-stations—Banagher, Rathdowney, Cloghan, Cullahill, and Clononey, which numbered 2 captains, 4 subalterns, 9 sergeants, 2 drummers, and 202 rank and file ; of these two companies were in Banagher, under the command of Captain Lodge. The light company was subsequently sent to Mountmellick.

From the arrival of the regiment at Birr and at its out-stations in November, 1815, nothing worthy of remark occurred until the latter end of February, 1816, when any leave of absence granted to officers by the commander of the forces from that time, was sure to be accompanied by a concluding paragraph, that "those officers must hold themselves in readiness to join upon orders being received for disembodying the regiment."

As the disembodying of the militia was now the fixed determination of the Government, routes were received by the officer commanding the Royal Tyrone Militia on the 11th of March, 1816, for the regiment to march in two divisions on the 14th and 15th of that month to Aughnacloy, according to the following arrangements :—

First division, commanded by Captain Kyffin, on the 14th of March—Grenadiers, Captain Richardson's, Captain Lodge's, Captain Brien's companies, and vacant company.

Second division, commanded by Major Irvine, on the 15th of March—Captain Moore's, Captain Pringle's, Captain Boyle's, Captain Miller's companies, and light company.

On the regiment arriving at Aughnacloy, and prior to its being disembodied, a court of enquiry, of which Lieut.-Colonel William Stewart was president, was held by order of Colonel the (first) Earl of Caledon, to investigate such claims as might be submitted by the men of the regiment for its consideration.

The men of the regiment being allowed fourteen days' pay at the disembodiment to enable them to proceed to their respective homes, officers in command of companies were to take their receipt for that amount and to submit those receipts to the commanding officer, agreeable to a form to be seen at the orderly room.

A regimental order, of which the following is a transcript, was issued at Aughnacloy on the 28th of March, 1816 :—

"Major General Burnet having ordered the regiment to be formed at seven o'clock to-morrow morning, for the purpose of being disembodied, the Earl of Caledon avails himself of this last opportunity of expressing to the officers, non-commissioned officers, and privates, the sense of obligation he entertains for the exemplary manner in which the regiment has conducted itself. The Earl of Caledon earnestly requests the soldiers to show their discipline to his orders by separating without noise or tumult, and he recommends them to return to their respective homes with as little delay as possible."

The following is a list of the officers serving with the Royal Tyrone Militia at its disembodiment on the 29th of March, 1816 ; on which reduction the lieutenants and assistant-surgeon were allowed 2s. 6d., and the ensigns 2s. per day, as a retiring allowance during life ; but were liable to serve again in case of a re-embodiment of the militia, or if the regiment was called up for training.

COLONEL—

The Earl of Caledon.

LIEUT.-COLONEL—

William Stewart.

MAJOR—

William Irvine.

CAPTAINS—

John Moore.
Jonathan W. Kyffin.
Robert Richardson.
Richard R. Lodge.
James Brien.
John Irvine.
William Pringle.
Andrew Millar.
Alexander Boyle.

LIEUTENANTS—

Ralph Macklin, Paymaster.
John Hyde.
Alexander Campbell.
Thomas Young.
Roger C. Anketell.
Thomas Olpherts.
J. G. Bouchier.
Edward Moore.

Alfred G. Richardson.
John Lindsay.
Sinclair Perry.
Robert Thompson.

ENSIGNS—

Samuel Jamieson.
Andrew Patterson.
William Maxwell.
John Byers.
Daniel Mansergh.
Richard Kyffin.
Robert George Falls.

ADJUTANT—

Richard Carey.

QUARTERMASTER—

William Martin.

PAYMASTER—

Ralph Macklin.

SURGEON—

John Sinclair.

ASSISTANT SURGEON—

Joseph H. Scott.

CHAPTER V.

THE permanent staff of the regiment, comprising the following number of officers, non-commissioned officers, and drummers paraded on the 30th of March, 1816, at half-past eleven o'clock, and carrying the regimental colours, proceeded by route to Caledon to be stationed there until further orders: 1 adjutant—Richard Carey ; 1 quartermaster—Wm. Martin ; 1 paymaster—Ralph Macklin ; 1 surgeon—John Sinclair ; 1 sergeant-major—Ely Taylor ; 1 quartermaster-sergeant—James Darragh ; 1 drum-major—John Thornton ; 40 sergeants, 50 corporals, and 20 drummers.

The large mansion formerly occupied by General Pringle's descendants, and which was then vacant, had been set apart by Lord Caledon for the resception of the four staff officers, with a splendid garden in its rere.

The office-houses of this mansion were nicely fitted up as barrack rooms for the accommodation of the other members of the staff, as also two other houses then known as " Waterloo," on the site of which the Caledon Mills were erected, and now stand.

Lord Caledon spared no expense in making those houses as comfortable as possible ; but the staff being so numerous all could not, be accommodated, and such married men as could not were permitted to provide themselves with houses in the town, or its vicinity.

His lordship being most anxious for the comfort and welfare of the staff, and particularly for the married men and their families, arranged with Quartermaster Martin to establish weaving shops for the employment of such men of the staff as had been brought up to that trade.

His lordship provided the looms, and Mr. Martin was to supply them with yarns of the different qualities for making the linens then in demand.

Such of the men as could not weave, and were willing to

work, were employed as labourers in his lordship's demesne.

However, these indulgences to the staff were not permitted to interfere with its military duties, either in the matter of parades, or guards.

A sergeant, two corporals, and a drummer mounted each day as barrack guard, in full dress, with arms and accoutrements.

Parades were held for Divine service, evening parades on Sundays with arms and accoutrements, and on each Monday morning throughout the spring and summer in fatigue dress, with arms and accoutrements, at six o'clock for drill in the demesne. All this was carried out until the 24th of December, 1822, when the staff was reduced by the discharge of fourteen sergeants, eighteen corporals, and five drummers.

On this reduction being carried out, the Earl of Caledon selected for discharge the senior sergeants who were entitled to pension from their long service. Measures being then in progress for extending the establishment of police in the Province of Munster, arrangements were made for attaching to it, as constables, such of the non-commissioned officers and drummers of the militia as might be discharged, provided they were qualified for such employment by being of sound constitution, able-bodied, under forty years of age, able to read and write, and of a good character for honesty, fidelity, and activity.

The corporals and drummers of the Tyrone, who availed themselves of this opportunity, were all approved of as being well qualified to act as constables ; one of the drummers named Moore rose to the rank of head-constable in a comparatively short time after joining that force.

I should have observed that in October, 1816, Surgeon John Sinclair retired on six shillings per day, and that his son, Alexander, succeeded him as surgeon on the staff of this regiment, his commission bearing date the 1st of November, 1816. He being removed to the medical staff in India in April, 1818, his uncle, Samuel Sinclair, suceeded him as surgeon on the staff of the Royal Tyrone.

Captain Carey having resigned the adjutancy of this regiment about the end of April, 1822, received a retiring allowance of eight shillings per day. The Earl of Caledon appointed Captain Richard R. Lodge to be adjutant, his commission bearing date the 2nd of May, 1822.

The following regimental order, issued by Colonel the Earl of Caledon, cannot fail to show the kind and benevolent disposition entertained by his lordship, and the anxiety he felt for the welfare of the families and staff under his lordship's command. I give the order, verbatim :—

"Caledon, 12th February, 1824.

"As several of the staff have lately died, leaving their families in great distress, Lord Caledon feels it necessary to call to the attention of those who remain, the duty they owe to themselves and their children of endeavouring to provide the means of future subsistence at a time when they are enabled to do so, as it is a fact that all the non-commissioned officers, with the advantages they enjoy, can save from their pay; and they should recollect that they are not only liable to the casualties to which all are subject, but that they are likewise liable to immediate reduction, or to a diminution of pay. Lord Caledon recommends when money is saved that it should be placed in a savings' bank, where it will bear interest, and may be withdrawn at any time. If Lord Caledon finds the advice neglected, he will suppose that the non-commissioned officers are deficient in frugality, and in this event, instead of allowing them to dissipate their time in idleness, as some appear to do, he will keep them employed in military duties—such as drills and guard mounting. In issuing this order, Lord Caledon is aware that some of the staff are industrious and educate their children —to such this order does not apply.

"CALEDON, Colonel."

In the beginning of the month of January, 1825, Surgeon Samuel Sinclair, who had been surgeon in the Royal Navy during the late war with France, and who, at its termination was placed on the temporary retired list, was now recalled to join that branch of the service, and the Earl of Caledon recommended the senior assistant-surgeon, Joseph H. Scott, as his successor, and on the 17th of January, 1825, his commission as surgeon was confirmed.

In the month of August, 1826, on the recommendation of his lordship, Captain Andrew Millar was appointed paymaster in succession to Captain William Pringle ; and in the month of May, 1827, Lieutenant John Hyde was appointed quartermaster on the decease of Mr. Martin.

The following extract, in reference to a further reduction of the staff of militia regiments, is taken from a war office circular of the 13th of January, 1829, No. 626.

"My Lord—I have the honor to inform your lordship that His Majesty's Government having taking into consideration the expense of the staff of the militia, have determined to submit to Parliament a bill for effecting some reduction in that branch of

L

the public expenditure.

" According to the proposed measure, the future establishment retained on permanent pay at headquarters will be for each corps —1 adjutant, 1 sergeant-major, 1 sergeant for every forty private men, 1 drummer for every two companies, with an additional drummer for each flank company; in addition to which, in regiments consisting of eight companies and upwards, a drum-major will be allowed.

" It is the intention of Government to reduce the following individuals, viz. : — paymasters, surgeons, quartermasters, quartermaster-sergeants, the number of sergeants exceeding the proportion of one for forty privates, all the corporals, the drum-majors of corps consisting of less than eight companies, the number of drummers exceeding one for every two companies, and one for each flank company, the two fifers of each regiment or battalion.

" You are therefore requested to furnish me as early as possible with a correct statement of the ages and services of all the individuals of these ranks, with a view to ascertain what reduced disembodied allowances any of them may be deemed to be entitled to."

The circular from which the foregoing extract is taken was addressed to Colonel the Earl of Caledon, and signed by H. Hardinge.

The reduction was carried out on the 24th of June, 1829, after which the regimental staff consisted of the adjutant, sergeant-major, drum-major, 16 sergeants, and 7 drummers ; but on the 10th day of October 1835, a further and last reduction took place, diminishing the staff to an adjutant, sergeant-major, and six sergeants, and if any of these died, or were discharged, the vacancy caused by either circumstance was not to be filled up.

The next circumstance I have to record in connection with the regiment is the lamented death of the first Earl of Caledon, which occurred in the month of April, 1839. His lordship had been colonel of the Royal Tyrone Militia for nearly 35 years, having succeeded the Earl of Belmore in command of the regi-ment on the 11th of August, 1804.

After his death, the late Earl of Caledon was appointed his successor on the 1st of May, 1839.

Captain Lodge, who had been adjutant of the regiment from the 2nd of May, 1822, in succession to Captain Carey, died on the 16th of September, 1840. This vacancy was not then filled up, pursuant to the Government order issued at the last reduction of the staff in October, 1835.

The next incident occurring with the diminished staff of the regiment was the appointment of Mr. Lundie, who had retired on pension from the Coldstream Guards, and whom Lord Caledon recommended for the adjutancy, in pursuance of a circular letter received from the war office, dated 1st December, 1845, of which the following is an extract :—

" Her Majesty having been graciously pleased to signify her commands that the permanent staff of the several regiments of militia in Ireland shall be completed to the number limited by the Act of the 5th and 6th of William the 4th, chap. 37, I have the honour to acquaint you that the establishment of the staff of the regiment under your command shall consist of the following numbers :—one adjutant, one sergeant-major, and eight sergeants."

On the 5th of March, 1846, Adjutant Lundie was appointed, but the two vacancies in the rank of sergeant were not filled up.

CHAPTER VI.

THE next circumstance in connection with the regiment is its re-embodiment, after a period of nearly thirty-nine years.

The Crimean war having been declared, a beating order was received by his lordship in the beginning of November, 1854, to raise volunteers for the regiment under his command.

In this matter his lordship, together with Lieut.-Colonel Stronge, took a most lively interest, and no doubt Lord Caledon then looked forward with some degree of pleasure to the time when he hoped to assume the command, and be found at the head of the regiment as its colonel.

During the months of November and December, 1854, and up to the 3rd of January, 1855, eighty-seven volunteers had been enrolled, but of this number sixteen had already extended their services to the line; so that on the morning of the 4th of January, 1855, the day named for assembling, there were only seventy-one mustered in the barrack yard at Caledon, independent of the staff.

The following are the names of officers present at the embodiment of the regiment, on the 4th of January, 1855, with the dates of their commissions :—

Rank and Name.	Date of Commission.	Remarks.
Colonel— The 2nd Earl of Caledon,	May, 1839	Previously in the regular army.
Lieut.-Colonel— James M. Stronge, ...	Oct., 1854	Previously in the regular army.
Major— Viscount Northland, ...	Jan., 1855	Resigned.
Captains— Robert M. Moore, ...	May, 1846	Resigned 3rd Feb. 1855.
Joseph Greer, ...	,,	Transferred to Tyrone Artillery.

List of Officers continued.

Rank and Name.	Date of Commission.	Remarks.
Burleigh Stuart, ...	May, 1846	Promoted major, March, 1861.
George W. Vesey, ...	,,	Transferred to Tyrone Artillery.
David White, ...	April, 1848	Resigned Dec. 28, 1857.
A. W. Cole Hamilton, ...	Nov., 1854	Promoted major, March, 1855.
Francis Ellis, ...	,,	Promoted major, April, 1862, now Hon. Lt.-Colonel.
James Galbraith, ...	,,	Died, 13th Oct., 1856.
Letablere J. Litton, ...	Dec., 1854	Resigned, 1856.
Martinus V. Bowie, ...	Jan., 1855	Resigned.
LIEUTENANTS—		
William Moore, ...	May, 1846	
Thomas Simpson, ...	,,	Resigned.
William H. Irwin, ...	,,	
Richard A. Shaw, ...	Mar., 1847	
Edward Moore, ...	Jan., 1852	
Richard White, ...	Sept., 1854	
Rowley Miller, ...	Oct., 1854	Resigned.
Luke F. Scott, ...	,,	
Abraham Anderson, ...	,,	
Lewis M. Buchanan, ...	Jan., 1855	
ENSIGNS—		
George Bourrieau, ...	May, 1846	
John Maxwell, ...	,,	
James Mayne, ...	Nov., 1854	
John M. Cochrane, ...	Dec., 1854	
Thomas A. Young, ...	,,	
John H. Maginnis, ...	,,	
Robert E. Sproule, ...	,,	Resigned.
Jackson Lloyd, ...	,,	
CAPTAIN AND ADJUTANT—		
William Lundie, ...	Mar., 1846	Resigned in '63, B. Major
QUARTERMASTER—		
John Core, ...	Jan., 1855	
SURGEON—		
Joseph H. Scott, ...	June, 1825	
ASSISTANT SURGEON—		
William Scott, ...	Jan., 1855	

After the assembly on the 4th of January, recruiting parties were sent out to the principal towns in the county for the purpose of enrolling volunteers, in which they succeeded admirably, as between the 4th and 30th of January, 77 recruits joined the regiment, but of these 15 went to the line, so that about 133 volunteers marched from Caledon to Omagh on the 30th, where they arrived on the 31st of January, 1855, a rather " motley group," as it was not possible to have them supplied with clothing in the meantime. However, they were not kept long in this state, as a heavy pressure was put upon Messrs. Dolan & Co., of London, the clothiers selected for the regiment, who soon after forwarded the necessary supplies of clothing.

No delay was now permitted to occur in sending out recruiting parties to the surrounding towns on market and fair days, and the success was so great that by the end of the month of June, the regiment was almost made up to 600 rank and file.

" Dublin Castle, 18th April, 1855.

" General Order—My Lord—I am directed by the Lord Lieutenant to inform your lordship in reference to your letter of the 16th ulto., that His Excellency has been pleased to direct that the Royal Tyrone Regiment of Militia shall bear the title of the Royal Tyrone Fusilier Regiment of Militia.

" I have the honor to be my lord,
" Your lordship's obedient servant,
" THOMAS A. LARCOM."

The Earl of Caledon, com-\
manding Royal Tyrone Fusilier }
Regiment of Militia.

" Headquarters, Omagh, 16th May, 1855.

" R. O.—Lieut.-Col. Stronge has much pleasure in making known to the regiment the general's entire approbation of their appearance and steadiness under arms, and the precision with which they executed all the manœvures at the inspection yesterday ; also the great satisfaction at their general good conduct and character, and that he will have much pleasure in reporting the same to the commander-in-chief."

" Headquarters, Omagh, 3rd July, 1855.

" R. O.—It is with the deepest regret that Lieutenant-Colonel Stronge has to announce to the Royal Tyrone Fusiliers that Colonel the Earl of Caledon died at his residence, Carlton Terrace, London, at nine o'clock on the morning of Saturday, the 30th June."

On the day of his lordship's funeral at Caledon, all the officers of the regiment, without exception, were present at that last sad ceremony, to see his remains deposited in their resting place.

Never shall the writer of this record forget the acts of kindness which his lordship manifested towards himself and his family on many occasions ; nor will he ever forget that it was by his influence that he has enjoyed for over seventeen years the honorable position of bearing Her Majesty's commission as an officer in the Royal Tyrone Fusiliers.

On the 10th of June, 1855, the regiment received the route for England, to which it was to proceed from Omagh by rail to Londonderry, in two divisions, on the 13th and 14th of July, and thence by steamer to Liverpool, and on by rail to Sheffield.

What a contrast will present itself to the mind of the reader of this record, on comparing the move of the regiment now from the county for the third time, with its first move on the 17th of March, 1794, to Waterford, and its second move to Limerick, in August, 1803 ! Then the marches were long and weary, with heavy knapsacks and well-filled pouches of ball-cartridge ; now there was nothing of this, as the men were neither foot-sore or wearied with heavy burdens, they and their baggage being carried by rail to their destination.

On the 4th of August following, a volunteering to the line took place in Sheffield, when 78 men of the Royal Tyrone Fusiliers extended their services to the following regiments :— to the Royal Artillery, 8 ; Royal Marines, 5 ; 7th Hussars, 6 ; Coldstream Guards, 15 ; 18th Royal Irish, 4 ; and the 68th, 40. As the result of this volunteering, Lieutenant Anderson was gazetted to the 44th foot, on the 6th of September, 1855.

"Headquarters, Sheffield, 17th October, 1855.

"R. O.—Lieutenant-Colonel Stronge has much pleasure in making known to the Royal Tyrone Fusiliers, Major-General Arbuthnot's entire approbation of their appearance under arms at his inspection yesterday.

"The steadiness, cleanliness, soldier-like appearance, and general good conduct of the regiment were particularly noticed by the general."

On the 20th of December, 1855, the regiment removed from Sheffield to Sunderland, as its headquarters, where seven companies were stationed, the remaining three companies being then sent on detachment to Tynemouth, under the command of Major Ross. On the 1st of January, 1856, No. 4 company was also sent to Tynemouth to augment the detachment there.

On the 15th of February, 1856, another volunteering from the Royal Tyrone Fusiliers to regiments of the line took place, when 86 men extended their services to the following corps :—

Royal Artillery, 30 ; Coldstream Guards, 2 ; 15th foot, 1 ; 21st, 3 ; 48th, 1 ; 69th, 1 ; 85th, 45 ; and Royal Marines, 3.

The regiment having again given such a large quota of volunteers to the line, Lieutenant L. M. Buchanan was gazetted ensign in the 88th regiment of foot on the 29th of February, 1856.

A destructive fire having occurred in the Lyceum Theatre at Sunderland on the morning of the 9th of March, 1856, on which occasion the regiment, with the barrack engine, was ordered out by Major Cole Hamilton, to assist in arresting its progress, the following resolution of the Town Council is recorded :—

" At a meeting of the Town Council of the Borough of Sunderland, held on Wednesday, the 12th day of March, 1856,

" Resolved unanimously—That the thanks of the Council be given to Major Hamilton, and the officers, and soldiers of the Royal Tyrone Fusiliers under his command, who assisted the police at the recent fire in the High-street, in this Borough, on the morning of the 9th instant, for their prompt, valuable, and efficient aid upon that occasion.

"ANTHONY JOHN MOORE, Mayor."

On the 22nd of May, 1856, the regiment was ordered to hold itself in readiness to move at short notice, and it was expected that it would be retained on Dublin duty for a time. On the morning of the 24th of May, it left Sunderland by rail for Whitehaven, where it arrived, and embarking the same evening on board the " Tynewald" steamer, sailed for the North Wall, Dublin, which it reached the following day. The regiment was disembarked under the superintendence of Colonel Doyle, then quartermaster-general, and, instead of remaining in Dublin as was expected, it was marched to the Amiens-street Station, where a train was in readiness to convey it to Armagh the same day, leaving a baggage guard under the command of Captain White, who, with the quartermaster, proceeded the following morning with it by rail to Armagh, where it was re-loaded on carts, and escorted by a guard under command of Lieutenant Maxwell to Omagh.

On arrival of the regiment at Omagh, one company was sent on detachment to Lifford.

"Headquarters, Omagh, 16th June, 1856.

" R. O.—Lieutenant-Colonel Stronge, commandant, has much pleasure in making known to the Royal Tyrone Fusiliers Major-General Gough's very great satisfaction on his inspection of the regiment this day. The major-general was pleased to express his entire approbation of the cleanliness and order of the barrack rooms, the good conduct of the men in quarters, their steadiness and soldier-like appearance under arms, and the precision with which they performed the different evolutions at the inspection. The major-general was also pleased to say that the good conduct of the men was a credit to themselves, their country, and the service generally."

The regiment was now disembodied for the third time on the 29th of August, 1856, after a service of a year and eight months.

The following is a list of the officers serving with the regiment at this disembodiment :—

Rank and Name.	Remarks.
LIEUTENANT-COLONEL—	
James M. Stronge.	
MAJORS—	
A. W. Cole Hamilton, ...	Promoted major, 19th March, 1855.
David R. Ross, ...	,, 4th July, 1855.
CAPTAINS—	
Burleigh Stuart,	
David White,	
Francis Ellis,	
James Galbraith,	
Andrew F. Knox, ...	Appointed 6th February, 1855.
Robert S. Lindesay, ...	,, 19th March, 1855.
Claud Houston, ...	,, 2nd June, 1855.
J. H. Armstrong, ...	,, 18th July, 1855.
William H. Irwin, ...	Promoted 6th March, 1856.
Edward C. Knox, ...	Appointed 12th April, 1856.
LIEUTENANTS—	
William Moore,	
Edward Moore,	
Richard White,	
Luke F. Scott,	
Deane Mann, ...	Appointed 27th January, 1855.
John Maxwell, ...	Promoted 21st February, 1855.
J. M. Cochran, ...	,, 29th February, 1856.
Thomas A. Young, ...	,, 6th March, 1856.
Joshua Pim, ...	Appointed 4th April, 1856.
John H. Maginnis, ...	Promoted 5th June, 1856.
ENSIGNS—	
James Wray, ...	Appointed 27th January, 1855.
Daniel Wilson, ...	,, 21st February, 1855.
Robert S. Hamilton, ...	,, 19th March, 1855.

M

List of Officers continued.

Rank and Name.	Remarks.
Robert W. Scott, ...	Appointed 30th April, 1855.
Barry Fox, ...	,, 1st June, 1855.
William G. Stack, ...	,, 13th September, 1855.
Francis W. Crossley, ...	,, 21st February, 1856.
Francis F. Robinson, ...	,, 11th April, 1856.
John B. M'Crea, ...	,, 5th June, 1856.
CAPTAIN AND ADJUTANT— ...way, ...	Appointed 16th February, 1855.
..STANT ..URGEON— ...t Moore, ...	,, ,, ,,
QUARTERMASTER— John Core.	
PAYMASTER— W. M. Carpendale, ...	,, 26th February, 1855.

As the permanent staff of the regiment was to be stationed in Dungannon after the disembodiment in August, the adjutant and quartermaster were directed by Lieutenant-Colonel Stronge to proceed there on the 28th of July, to make arrangements for proper store-rooms in which to preserve the clothing and accoutrements of the regiment. These rooms were provided at the expense of the county, and the arrangements being carried out, the staff moved from Omagh to Dungannon on the 1st of September, 1856, where it only remained for a little over twelve months, when the regiment was again ordered to be embodied in consequence of the Indian mutiny, and the staff to return to Omagh. On the 3rd day of November, 1857, the regiment re-assembled under the command of Lieutenant-Colonel Stronge.

The regiment having re-assembled at twelve o'clock on the 3rd of November, pursuant to the warrant of His Excellency the Lord Lieutenant, the following number of officers and men were present at the muster on that day:—3 field officers, 9 captains, 15 subalterns, 5 staff officers, 30 sergeants, and 433 drummers, rank and file.

On the 11th of November, 1857, routes were received for the regiment to march to Armagh in five divisions, of two companies each, the first to move on the following day, Thursday, the

12th ; the second on Friday, the 13th ; the third on Saturday, the 14th ; the fourth on Monday, the 16th ; and the fifth on Tuesday, the 17th of November. This march occupied three days, the first to Ballygawley, second to Caledon, and the third to Armagh, independent of the halt day, Sunday ; the second division was in Caledon, and the third in Ballygawley.

The regiment only remained about a month in Armagh, when a route was received for its removal to Hamilton, in Lanarkshire.

It proceeded by rail from Armagh to Belfast on the 15th of December, and thence by the steamer "Elk" to Glasgow ; a second steamer followed with the baggage, in charge of the quartermaster, with a guard under the command of Lieutenant William Moore. On arriving at Glasgow, the regiment marched to the railway station, and proceeded to Hamilton, with the exception of Nos. 3 and 9 companies, which were sent on detachment to Paisley, under command of Major Ross. Two other companies, Nos. 4 and 5, were ordered to Paisley on the 2nd of April, 1858.

Volunteering to the line having taken place on the 22nd of February and 16th of April, 1858, 49 men of the Royal Tyrone Fusiliers extended their services to various regiments, which are not enumerated.

Major-General Viscount Melville having notified his intention to Lieutenant-Colonel Stronge that he would inspect the regiment on the 22nd of April, 1858, at Hamilton, and having carried out that intention, the result was communicated to the officers and men in the following complimentary terms : " Lieutenant-Colonel Stronge, commandant, has much pleasure in making known to the regiment Major-General Lord Melville's approbation and entire satisfaction with the soldier-like bearing of the officers and men under arms, and with the steadiness and precision with which they executed every movement during the major-general's inspection this morning, and with the high character and general good conduct of the regiment."

It having been again determined by the Government to dis-embody the militia of the United Kingdom, a letter was received from Dublin Castle, bearing date the 22nd of April, 1858, from which I extract the following paragraphs :—

" Sir—I am commanded by the Lord Lieutenant to request that the general commanding will convey to the commanding officers of the several corps which are to be disembodied, the expression of the very great satisfaction which Her Majesty has reeceived from the exemplary services of the corps under their command, and to acquaint you that Her Majesty is pleased to grant the following allowances on the occasion to the officers and men hereinafter mentioned :—

"To each subaltern, an allowance equal to six months' pay, and to the surgeon and assistant-surgeon, an allowance equal to one year's pay, from the day of disembodiment, exclusive.

"The adjutant and other members of the permanent staff are not to have any gratuity or allowance on disembodiment, as they will revert to the pay fixed for their respective ranks previously to the embodiment of the corps, as specified in Article 186 of the Militia Regulations, dated the 1st September, 1854. The quartermaster, now holding a commission as such, will also be retained on the permanent staff, with pay at 5s. per diem.

"His Excellency desires, in conclusion, to express the satisfaction which he feels in having the honour of signifying on the present occasion Her Majesty's gracious approbation of the services of the officers, non-commissioned officers, drummers, and private men belonging to the regiment about to be disembodied.

"THOMAS A. LARCOM."

The regiment having now received the route for Omagh, the first division of five companies left Hamilton at half-past twelve o'clock on the 6th of May, by rail to Glasgow, and embarked on board the steamer " Rose" for Londonderry ; the remaining five companies left at the same hour on the 8th, for Glasgow, and embarked on board the " Thistle," for same place, arriving in Omagh from Londonderry on the 9th of May, 1858.

CHAPTER VII.

    LL that I now think necessary to notice with regard to the officers is the few changes which took place since the disembodiment in 1856, and these are as follows :—

Captain E. R. F. Stronge, appointed 16th October, 1857, Sir J. M. Stewart, resigned; Captain George W. Vesey, appointed 29th December, 1857, Captain D. White, resigned; Lieutenant Daniel Wilson, promoted 10th February, 1857, J. M. Cochran, resigned; Lieutenant George P. M'Clintock, appointed 10th February, 1857, J. H. Maginnis, resigned; Ensign William Porter, appointed 21st Nov., 1857, G. K. Horner, resigned; Ensign Edward Stack, appointed 29th November, 1857, F. W. Crossley, resigned; Ensign J. R. Baillie, appointed 15th Jan., 1858, Daniel Wilson, promoted.

From the 15th of May up to the 23rd of August, 1858, sixty-three volunteers of the regiment joined different regiments of the line, for which purpose they obtained their release from their militia engagement, and fifty-four more extended their services from that date up to the 9th of April, 1859.

Major A. W. Cole Hamilton having resigned his commission, he was succeeded by Major James Alfred Caulfeild, on the 10th of June, 1859.

On the 15th of July, 1859, the regiment was called up for twenty-one days' training and exercise, and on the 2nd of August it was inspected by Colonel W. Hamilton, C.B., after which the following appeared in orders—" The commandant, Lieutenant Colonel Stronge, has much pleasure in making known to the officers and men of the Royal Tyrone Fusiliers the entire approbation of the inspecting field-officer, Colonel W. Hamilton, C.B., of the appearance of the regiment at his inspection this morning, and also of the very good conduct of the men in quarters during the period of training."

16th November, 1859.—Captain Lundie, with Sergeant Scoles and Sergeant Donaghy, having been ordered to the School of

Musketry at Hythe, the charge of the staff, and the carrying out of the enrolment duty devolved upon the quartermaster during the absence of the adjutant.

On the 23rd of December, 1858, Captain Andrew F. Knox, of the Royal Tyrone Fusiliers, exchanged regiments with Captain C. K. Colhoun of the Donegal Milltia ; and on the 19th of July, 1859, Lieutenant Deane Mann was promoted to be captain, in room of Captain Vesey, who resigned ; and on the 4th of February, 1860, Lieutenant George P. M'Clintock was promoted to be captain, in succession to Captain Edmund R. F. Stronge, resigned ; Ensign Robert S. Hamilton was promoted to be lieutenant the 29th April, 1859, in the room of Edward Moore, transferred to the Gold Coast Corps ; Ensign Robert W. Scott promoted to be lieutenant the 19th July, 1859, in room of Lieutenant Dean Mann ; and Ensign J. B. M'Crea promoted on the 15th September, in succession to Lieutenant Luke F. Scott, appointed to the 1st Royal Regiment of foot.

The regiment having been ordered to assemble for training on the 21st of May, 1860, it was removed for that purpose to Enniskillen on the 23rd, to occupy the barracks there during the period for which it was embodied.

The regiment was inspected by Colonel H. Doyle on the 11th of June, after which the following communication by regimental order was promulgated—" The commandant, Lieut.-Colonel Stronge, has much gratification in making known to the regiment the inspector-general's entire approbation with its appearance at his inspection this morning, their cleanliness, and the manner in which they executed all the different manœuvres and movements required by him from the regiment, and which were performed in a manner beyond what he could have expected, and their conduct during the training was worthy of the highest commendation."

On the 16th of May, 1861, the volunteers who had been enrolled from the termination of the training in 1860 were ordered in for fourteen days' drill previous to the general assembly of the regiment.

These were under the command of Captain (now Brevet Lieut.-Colonel) Ellis, and Lieutenants Maxwell and Young, who were to superintend the drilling of them in conjunction with the adjutant.

On the 30th of May, the remainder of the regiment assembled in Omagh Barracks, and having been clothed and fully equipped, it proceeded again this year to Enniskillen on the 31st of May, for training and exercise, having barrack accommodation there.

On the 19th of June, 1861, Major-General Doyle inspected the regiment at Enniskillen, when his praise of it was again communicated by regimental order in the following terms :— " The commandant, Lieutenant-Colonel Stronge, has much pleasure in making known to the regiment Major-General Doyle's entire approbation and approval of the appearance of the Royal Tyrone Fusiliers at his inspection this morning, the cleanly appearance, and general good conduct of the men, considering the short time they have been assembled. The zeal of officers and non-commissioned officers drew from Major-General Doyle the highest commendations, and gave him great pleasure to make known to the regiment that he would not fail to report the high condition he found them in to the Lord Lieutenant of Ireland."

Captain Burleigh Stuart was promoted to the rank of major on the 23rd of March, 1861, in room of Major Ross, resigned.

Major-General Doyle's staff appointment having terminated, he was succeeded by Colonel Smyth as Inspector-General of the Irish militia, who, on the 27th of November, 1861, inspected the staff at Omagh Barracks, after which he instructed Captain Lundie to make known to the men his entire approbation of their soldier-like and military appearance on his inspection that day, together with the cleanliness of the stores and barracks.

" Headquarters, Omagh, 25th April, 1862.

" The Right Honorable the Earl of Charlemont has been pleased to make the following promotions and appointments in the Royal Tyrone Fusiliers, viz :—Lieutenant-Colonel J. M. Stronge to honorary colonel, to date from 22nd April ; Major James A. Caulfeild to be lieutenant-colonel, vice Lieutenant-Colonel Stronge appointed honorary colonel; Captain Francis Ellis to be major, vice Major Caulfeild promoted, to date from 22nd April, 1862."

The usual notice of assembly having been forwarded to the addresses of the volunteers in April, 1862, and the recruits who had been enrolled since last training ordered in for fourteen days' preliminary drill prior to the general assembling of the regiment, one captain and one subaltern were authorized to assist the adjutant in this duty. On this occasion Captain M'Clintock and Lieutenant Wilson were selected.

The regiment having assembled for twenty-one days' training and exercise on the 4th of June, on the 5th the following appeared in regimental orders :—" In accepting the rank of honorary colonel, and thereby retiring from the direct command of the Royal Tyrone Fusiliers, Colonel Stronge is desirous to express to the regiment the deep sense he entertains of its excellent conduct during the period he had the honour of having it under his command as lieutenant-colonel, and it always will be a great gratification to him to feel that he still belongs to a corps which has been so eminently distinguished for discipline and efficiency, a character he is confident it will ever continue to maintain."

"Headquarters, Omagh, 19th June, 1862.

"Lieutenant-Colonel Caulfeild, commanding, has much pleasure in conveying to the regiment, in regimental orders, how highly gratified Colonel E. S. Smyth, Inspector-General of Militia, felt at the very creditable inspection this morning. He referred to the steadiness of the men under arms, and especially to their general good conduct in quarters. He was pleased to say that the state of the regiment reflected the highest credit on the officers, non-commissioned officers, and privates, and that he would not fail to make a most favourable report of their efficiency to Her Majesty's Government."

"Headquarters, Omagh, 24th June, 1862.

"The commanding officer has much pleasure in making known to the regiment the following letter received from the stipendiary magistrate, R. D. Coulson, Esq., and takes this opportunity of publishing the same in orders, for the information of the officers, non-commissioned officers, and men of the regiment :—

"Omagh, 24th June, 1862.

"My Dear Colonel Caulfield—Allow me to congratulate you upon the peaceable and orderly conduct of your regiment while embodied for training here. My brother magistrates join me in conveying to you, the officers, and men, our high appreciation. It is in truth a most creditable thing to the men that, with nearly 900 of them in billets, there was no disturbance of the public peace, nor anything that the local authorities could complain of, but all well conducted.

"With best wishes,
"Believe me sincerely yours,
R. D. COULSON, R.M."

On the 1st of June, 1863, the usual preliminary drill of 14 days for recruits commenced, when Captain L. M. Buchanan, who had been appointed on the 4th of July, 1862, and Lieut. Maxwell were selected to assist the adjutant in this duty, and on the 15th of June the regiment assembled for 21 days' training and exercise in Omagh.

1st July, 1863.—"The Inspector-General of Militia having

this day inspected the Royal Tyrone Fusiliers, wishes to convey to them in regimental orders his satisfaction with their clean appearance and steadiness under arms ; and the reports which have reached him of their excellent conduct in billets are most creditable to the regiment, and he hopes it may continue until the end of the training, which will enable him to make a most favourable report of the corps to His Excellency the Lord Lieutenant of Ireland, and to Her Majesty's Government."

Captain Lundie having resigned the adjutancy of the Royal Tyrone Fusiliers on the 1st of October, 1863, His Excellency the Lord Lieutenant was pleased to confer on him the rank of brevet-major, and at the same time appointed R. C. D. Ellis, late captain in Her Majesty's 22nd regiment of foot, to be adjutant in succession to Captain Lundie.

The regiment was trained in Omagh in the years of 1864 and 1865, and with the same result as on former occasions. It was remarkable for the cleanliness, steadiness under arms, and general good conduct of the men.

Fenianism having now unmasked itself, spread rapidly through various parts of Ireland. All kinds of depredations were committed, police stations were attacked—the arms in some instances carried away—and several agrarian outrages perpetrated. Under these appalling circumstances of the kingdom, the authorities in Dublin Castle considered it absolutely necessary to use every precaution in protecting the military stores in charge of the militia staffs, and for this purpose a circular was issued by the Inspector-General, on the 23rd Sept., 1865, to the Royal Tyrone Fusiliers, to mount a guard consisting of three sergeants and a drummer, daily, until further orders. A number of bags were also supplied, which were to be filled with sand, and kept in the guard-room for the purpose of extinguishing "Greek fire," should any of this destructive material be used. These guards were continued all throughout the winter of 1865, and up till the 15th of April, 1866.

This disaffection and disloyalty to Her Majesty's Government prevented the Irish Militia from being called out for training from 1865 to the year 1871. And although the loyal province of Ulster suffered indignity in this respect, in common with the other provinces, yet, as it would have been invidious to have made any distinction, I am persuaded that the Government acted wisely in this matter.

But the suspension of the training of the Irish Militia was not the only evil Fenianism produced. There was another, and that was the prohibition of the enrolment of volunteers, so that

N

the militia regiments were greatly reduced in number by not having the privilege to enrol men to replace those who were released from their militia engagements to serve in regiments of the line, as well as those whose periods of service had expired. Under these circumstances, it required the utmost exertion on the part of militia adjutants, when this prohibition was removed, to obtain volunteers to make up the necessary deficiencies.

The guard over the regimental stores was resumed on the 1st of December, 1866, and was continued through the winter and spring months of 1867, 1868, and 1869, and from the 17th of January, 1870, until the 22nd of June following; but during this latter period there were only two sergeants and a drummer on daily duty.

Colonel Smyth, Inspector-General, having notified to Captain Ellis that he would inspect the staff of the Royal Tyrone Fusiliers on the 18th of January, 1867, it was ordered to parade in heavy marching order on that day, at 2.30 p.m., and when the inspection was over, Colonel Smyth was so pleased that he complimented the adjutant on the cleanliness, efficiency, and the soldier-like appearance of the men of the permanent staff, and having examined the regimental and quartermaster's books, proceeded to inspect the stores, accompanied by the adjutant and quartermaster, and expressed himself well pleased with the state in which he found the clothing and accoutrements of the regiment kept.

Colonel Smyth's term of service as Inspector-General of the Irish militia having terminated, Colonel Maude, C.B.V.C., late of the 3rd Buffs, was appointed to succeed him. On the 3rd of December, 1867, he visited Omagh to inspect the permanent staff.

As on former occasions of inspection, the staff paraded in heavy marching order, and underwent a close and minute inspection of their clothing and appointments, the state of which pleased the inspector-general. Subsequently, he tested the efficiency of the sergeants singly in squad and company drill, and the drummers in sounding the bugle calls. After the inspection he proceeded to the orderly room to examine the regimental books, and finally ended his inspection in the regimental stores. He expressed himself well pleased with the cleanliness and soldier-like appearance of the staff, and also with the state of the stores.

His Royal Highness Prince Arthur having arrived at the Viceregal Lodge, on a visit to His Excellency Earl Spencer, in

1869, and taking a tour northward to visit the Maiden City, Portrush, and the Giant's Causeway, left Dublin on the 28th of April, accompanied by Lieutenant-Colonel Caulfeild, commandant of the Royal Tyrone Fusiliers, and arrived at the Omagh Station of the Ulster Railway by mid-day train. Captain Ellis, being apprised of the coming of His Royal Highness, was present at the railway station with the staff as a guard of honor, accompanied by Captains M'Clintock, Buchanan, and Auchinleck, with the Queen's colours.

His Royal Highness having to wait the arrival of the train of the Irish North-Western Railway from Enniskillen, to convey him to Derry, left his carriage, attended by Lieutenant-Colonel Caulfeild, and inspected the staff on the platform.

On the 29th of April the following appeared in staff orders on that date:—" His Royal Highness Prince Arthur Patrick having inspected the permanent staff of the Royal Tyrone Fusiliers, while on guard of honor at Omagh, has much pleasure in expressing his high opinion of their smart and soldier-like appearance.

" The general good conduct of the regiment, which Colonel Caulfeild has brought to His Royal Highness' notice, is most satisfactory and creditable not only to the men themselves, but also to the fine county they represent.

" By order,
" R. C. D. ELLIS, Captain and Adjutant,
" Royal Tyrone Fusiliers."

It having been determined by Her Majesty's Government that the Irish Militia should be called up for fifty-six days' traning, a beating order was issued by His Excellency the Lord Lieutenant on the 4th of January, 1871, for the purpose of enrolling volunteers for the Royal Tyrone Fusiliers.

On receipt of this order, Captain Ellis set to work most vigorously, visiting almost all the towns and villages in the county on market and fair days, and by the unwearied exertions of himself and the members of the staff who accompanied him, succeeded in raising no less than four hundred and thirty-six volunteers between the 4th of January and the 4th of May, 1871. These volunteers having assembled on the 4th of May for twenty-one days' preliminary drill, previous to the general assembly, Captain Buchanan and Lieutenants Charles M. Alexander and Henry Irvine were ordered to join, to assist the adjutant in performing this duty.

The remainder of the regiment assembled on the 25th of May, and although six years had elapsed since last training, they made rapid progress in their drill, through the care bestowed upon their instruction by both officers and non-commissioned officers.

On the evening of the 12th of June, His Excellency the Lord Lieutenant, with his private secretary and aids-de-camp, arrived at Omagh from Lifford, where he had been inspecting the Donegal and Derry regiments.

He was met at the Omagh Station by Colonel Caulfeild and a guard of honor, consisting of a company of the Royal Tyrone Fusiliers, under the command of Captain Colhoun and Lieutenants Charles and Henry Alexander, carrying the Queen's colours.

On the following day, Tuesday the 13th of June, the Fermanagh Light Infantry, under the command of Lieutenant-Colonel Archdall, arrived by train from Enniskillen, and was brigaded with the Royal Tyrone Fusiliers for the inspection of His Excellency.

After the inspection of both regiments, and marching past, they went through all the evolutions and movements of a review, after which both regiments formed in three sides of a square, when they were addressed by His Excellency as follows :—

" Colonel Caulfeild, officers, and men of the Fermanagh Light Infantry and Royal Tyrone Fusiliers—I have been visiting different parts of this country to see the militia regiments, and I was most anxious to come to this part of Ireland, where military traditions are so great, and where men have always distinguished themselves. I come, as the representative of the Queen, to thank you all for having joined the militia, a force of so much importance to the country. It is satisfactory on this the first occasion of their reassembling to find so many men rejoining the regiment, and so many recruits entering the ranks. I have reviewed with great pleasure militia regiments in other parts of the country, and I have observed with gratification the orderly conduct of the men, who have in all cases behaved themselves as soldiers should. The Tyrone Fusiliers which I have now reviewed are not surpassed in efficiency by any other regiment in Ireland. The county is a large one, and I am happy to see the ranks well filled. The other regiment, the Fermanagh Light Infantry, comes from a smaller county, and has fewer men, but its movements are distinguished by military precision. On previous occasions both regiments have sent men into the regular army, and I feel confident that should the Queen again require volunteers, Her Majesty will find no more loyal soldiers than the men of the Fermanagh and Tyrone Militias. You will now return to your homes, having learned the art of war, and important duties as citizens. I again thank you most heartily for having joined the militia, for the proficiency you have made in your drill, and for the admirable manner in which you have conducted yourselves."

His Excellency honoured the colonel and officers of the Royal Tyrone Fusiliers by dining with them at their mess, on the evenings of the 12th and 13th of June, accompanied by his private secretary and aids-de-camp. Numerous invitations were given to the noblemen and gentry of the county to meet His Excellency. The following guests were present at dinner :— The Earl of Enniskillen ; Colonel Archdall, Fermanagh Light Infantry ; Colonel Conyngham, Londonderry Light Infantry ; Major Stuart ; Captain Cardew, staff officer of pensioners ; and officers of the Donegal Militia and Artillery, etc., etc.

On the 23rd of June, the regiment was inspected by Colonel Armstrong, C.B., deputy adjutant-general, at the termination of which he addressed the regiment in the following terms :—

" Colonel Caulfeild, officers, non-commissioned officers, and men of the Royal Tyrone Fusiliers—Before I allude to any other subject, I wish first of all to express to you the great satisfaction with which I have heard of your good conduct since you have been called out for training. You have not had the advantage of barracks, but have been billeted through your town, notwithstanding which, your conduct has been reported to me as having been in every respect excellent, and such as no line regiment could excel. And now with regard to your military efficiency. In coming to inspect you to-day, you have laboured under one disadvantage, that is, that I heard from officers of much military experience that your regiment had attained a considerable degree of efficiency, and my expectations regarding you were therefore proportionally great. Notwithstanding this, I have not been disappointed. I am not going to say that you are equal to any regiment in the regular army, for that is not to be expected ; but I do say in all honesty that no regiment or portion of Her Majesty's troops brought together for the first time could have shown more steadiness under arms, or have acquired a greater knowledge of drill in the same limited time. This shows to me clearly that your heart has been in the work, and that you have seconded the efforts of your officers and non-commissioned officers, and have with them taken a proper pride in your duties. It is most creditable that you should in so short a time have attained so much proficiency, as is manifested in the manner in which you have gone through the movements, whether of battalion, light infantry, or the manual exercise. I cannot forget, however, that you have the advantage of being commanded by an old officer of the guards, regiments that are a pattern to the service. I observe that your great coats are well folded, and your packs well put on, and carried with an ease that can only be acquired by men accustomed to manœuvres with them on ; and I feel assured that next year, or at some early period, when your new clothing, accoutrements, and head dresses have been supplied to you, and you have had another year's training, this regiment, whether in appearance or proficiency, will equal any regiment in Her Majesty's forces. I have said to your comrades of the Derry Light Infantry what I now say to you.

"I have always, since I have been a soldier, maintained that the militia is the most valuable nursery for the British army.

"Referring to history, even at Waterloo the militia played a most important part. It has been said that many of the troops which took part in that great battle were recruits, but if they were, they were from the militia, some of them even in the uniform of their old regiments, and from their training they were able to stand before the greatest army, commanded by the greatest general France ever produced.

"At a later period—during the Russian war—they furnished valuable additions to the army, of which I have personal knowledge.

"I have no hesitation in expressing my opinion of the superiority of such men as I see before me over the mere boys generally supplied to the army.

"Colonel Caulfeild, you ought to be proud of your regiment ; and I feel confident they will do their duty in a manner worthy of their country. should they ever be called upon.

"I shall have great pleasure in making a most favorable report of them to His Excellency the Lord Lieutenant."

Having thus brought this record of the Royal Tyrone Fusilier Regiment of Militia from the year 1793 up to its training in the past year, 1871, it has afforded me the most unmixed pleasure to find that amongst the many officers and men of His Majesty's forces who were tried at various times for mutiny, sedition, and disloyalty to the Crown by courts martial, neither officer nor soldier of the Royal Tyrone was ever impeached with, nor accused of either or any of these crimes.

It was always remarkable for its loyalty, and was applauded by the generals and officers under whom it served for this distinguished character, as the reader of this record will have found.

I would add, in conclusion, that I feel proud in belonging to a regiment which has always been conspicuous for its loyalty and attachment to the Crown and Constitution of the country, and if the reader derives an equal pleasure from the perusal of this record as I did in my humble but earnest efforts in collecting and putting it together, I shall feel amply rewarded.

APPENDIX.

LIST OF OFFICERS.

Headquarters—Omagh, 1872.

Length of Service in the regiment	Rank and Name.	Date of Present Commission.
Yrs.	HONORARY COLONEL—	
17	Sir James Matthew Stronge, Bart, J.P., D.L., late 5th Dragoon Guards, ...	April 22, 1862
	LIEUT.-COLONEL COMMANDANT—	
13	*James Alfred Caulfeild, J.P., D.L., late Lieut. and Capt. Coldstream Guards,	April 22, 1862
	MAJORS—	
17	Francis Ellis, J.P., Hon. Lt.-Col., ...	April 22, 1862
15	George Perry M'Clintock, J.P., D.L., ...	Feb. 8, 1871
	CAPTAINS—	
16	†John Herbert Armstrong, Hon. Major, late Lieut. 95th Foot, ...	July 17, 1855
13	Charles King Colhoun, ...	Dec. 23, 1858
17	Deane Mann, J.P., ...	July 19, 1859
9	‡William Cole Hamilton, late Captain 88th Foot, ...	June 20, 1862
9	‖Lewis Mansergh Buchanan, late Lieut. 88th Foot, ...	June 20, 1862
16	Robert Saunderson Hamilton, ...	June 10, 1864
9	Hon. Robert Torrens O'Neill, ...	June 15, 1865
6	§Thomas Auchinleck, J.P., late 11th Foot,	June 16, 1865
	M. V. H. Gledstanes, late Lieut. 57th Foot, ...	Sept. 7, 1871
	¶Lord George F. Hamilton, late Lieut. Coldstream Guards, ...	Oct. 25, 1871
	LIEUTENANTS—	
15	John Benjamin M'Crea, ...	Sept. 15, 1859
7	Alexander Oliver S. M'Causland, ...	June 10, 1864
1	Charles M. Alexander, ...	Jan. 3, 1871

List of Officers continued.

Length of Service in the regiment	Rank and Name.	Date of Present Commission.
1	Houston French, P.S., ...	Jan. 3, 1871
1	Henry Irvine, ...	Jan. 25, 1871
1	James M. Stronge, ...	March 10, 1871
1	Henry G. S. Alexander, ...	March 10, 1871
1	Rowley A. Miller, ...	April 14, 1871
1	John B. Thompson, ...	April 14, 1871
1	William Anketell, ...	May 17, 1871
1	Hon. Charles Alexander (supern.), ...	Sept. 7, 1871
1	Hon. M. H. H. M'Donnell (supern.), ...	Sept. 7, 1871
	ADJUTANT AND CAPTAIN—	
8	**Robert Conway Dobbs Ellis, late Capt. 22nd Foot, ...	Oct. 1, 1863
	PAYMASTER—	
17	William Maxwell Carpendale, ...	Feb. 26, 1855
	QUARTERMASTER—	
59	John Core, ...	Jan. 17, 1855
	SURGEON—	
17	John Moore, M.D., ...	April 14, 1860
	ASSISTANT-SURGEON—	
1	Edward C. Thompson, M.B., ...	May 17, 1871

*Lieutenant-Colonel Caulfeild served in China from 1851 to 1853, with the 59th regiment. In the Crimean campaign with the Coldstream Guards, including the trenches before Sevastopol from November, 1854, until the fall of the town, and was present at the attack on the enemy's works on the 18th of June. Was invalided to Scutari Hospital, and thence to England in October, 1855. Rejoined his regiment in the Crimea in January, 1856, served with it until the close of the war, and returned with the batallion to England in July following.
(Medal and Clasp, and Turkish Medal).

†Captain Armstrong, Hon. Major, served in China from 1847 to 1850, with the 95th regiment, and retired in the year, 1852.

‡Captain William C. Hamilton served in India from November, 1852, to May, 1855, with the 8th King's Regiment. Was promoted to the 88th Connaught Rangers, and served with it in

Malta. Was placed on half pay after the Crimean war, for one year, and after that period rejoined the 88th regiment, and served with it till May, 1858, when he retired.

‖Captain Lewis M. Buchanan served with the 88th Connaught Rangers from 1856 till 1862. He embarked at Portsmouth with the headquarters of the regiment in July, 1857, for India, arriving there at an early stage of the mutiny, through which he served in the field till its final suppression. He was present at the repulse of the Gwalior Rebels at the Pandoo Nuddee, in November, 1857, the battles of the 27th and 28th November at Subahdar's Tank, (specially reported as having on that occasion shot three of the enemy with his revolver), and the operations from the entrenchments outside Cawnpore, resulting in the complete defeat of the enemy by Lord Clyde on the 6th December. Upon the formation of the Cawnpore Flying Column, he was appointed orderly officer by Brigadier Maxwell, C.B., commanding, and served in the various operations in the Doab ; was present at the capture of Lucknow, in March, 1858, and from that period till May in the operations of the same column, in conjuction with the central India Field Force, under Sir Hugh Roe, including the siege and capture of Calpie, and afterwards till the termination of the Hot Weather campaign. Was present with the regiment at Lucknow from the following October, and in various operations in Oude, disarming villages and dismantling forts till the regiment marched for Delhi, in February, 1859, when he served with it till appointed to the Laudour Depôt (Himalayas) in May, 1860, whence he returned to England in 1861, and retired in 1862.

(Indian Medal and Clasp).

§Captain Thomas Auchinleck served in the Cape of Good Hope with the 2nd battalion of the 11th regiment from June, 1861, till March, 1862. Was promoted lieutenant in the first battalion of the 11th, and retired in January, 1865.

¶Lord George F. Hamilton served in Canada with the Prince Consort's Own Rifle Brigade.

**Adjutant and Captain Robert Conway Dobbs Ellis served with the 22nd regiment in Malta, from 21st May, 1860, up to June, 1863, when he retired.

Officers who have retired from the regiment with authority to retain honorary rank for length of service :—

Date.	Name.		Rank.
1859, June 19,	Arthur W. C. Hamilton,	...	Major.
1863, October 1	William Lundie, ...	...	Major.
1871, Feb. 8	Burleigh Stuart, ...	...	Major.
,,	John Maxwell, ...	...	Major.

DETAILS OF MURDER IN TRALEE.

I am indebted to Lieutenant-Colonel Ellis for a copy of the *Kerry Evening Post* of the 28th of February, 1872, from which I extract the following valuable information relative to the murder of this man, who was named William Currans, shot, while standing a sentinel on the Custom House at Tralee, on the morning of the 21st December, 1797 :—

(From *Chute's Western Herald*, Tralee. Friday, Dec. 22, 1797.)

"A base and horrible murder, attended with circumstances of the most cowardly and premeditated villany, we are shocked to say, was perpetrated in this town, between the hours of one and two of the clock on the morning of yesterday, the 21st instant :—As William Currans, a private soldier of the Royal Tyrone Regiment of Militia, was standing sentinel on the Custom House, he was accosted by a person in woman's attire, who, after having answered his challenge with the usual response, requested to know the hour of the night, &c., and after a few more cursory words of conversation, passed along the Quay. The soldier, in a few seconds after, hearing footsteps approach the rere of his box (towards the river), immediately stepped out, and perceived the same person quite close to him, who, on the instant, fired a pistol, a ball from which, entering the inside of the sentinel's thigh, and, having lacerated a principal blood-vessel, passed out a few inches above his knee. The perfidious assassin immediately fled, and though the wounded soldier returned the fire as soon as he possibly could, we are sorry to say it was without effect. The shots having alarmed the Collector and his family, the unfortunate man was found wallowing in his blood, and though the assistance of an eminent surgeon was procured as speedily as possible, so great was the hemorrhage, that he expired about five o'clock yesterday morning, having just time minutely to relate the circumstances attending this deed of horror. This melancholy catastrophe is rendered still more dismal by having the unhappy wife and family of this ill-fated victim of cruelty thus suddenly deprived of their sole support ! !

We cannot dismiss this article without once more expressing our abhorrence and utter detestation of this treacherous act of wanton and unprovoked villany ; and we sincerely hope that the act of a barbarous midnight ruffian will not, in the eyes of our countrymen, be deemed a cause sufficient for fixing a stigma on this loyal and peaceable county, the more especially, as we are well convinced we speak the honest sentiment of every well-informed and unprejudiced individual in this town and neighbourhood, when we, thus publicly, offer the well-merited tribute of applause to the Royal Tyrone Militia, whose conduct has been, on all occasions (much to their honour), not only orderly and decorous, but in every sense of the word, *in the highest degree* exemplary."

MURDER ! !

Deeply impressed with a just abhorrence of the dreadful crime of assassination, determined by every effort in our power to bring the perpetrator of so atrocious a deed to condign punishment, and anxious to preserve the character for peace and good order which has hitherto distinguished this town and its neighbourhood, we, the Provost and inhabitants of the town of Tralee and its vicinity, whose names are hereunto subscribed, do hereby promise to pay the sums to our names respectively annexed, for discovering and prosecuting to conviction, within six calendar months of the date hereof, the person or persons concerned in the murder of William Currans, a private in the Royal Tyrone Regiment of Militia, while on duty as sentinel on the Custom House in Tralee, early on the morning of the 21st December, 1797 :—

	£	s.	d.		£	s.	d.
Glanmore ...	22	15	0	John Hurly ...	2	5	6
Sutton Frizell, for R.				Thomas Chute ...	2	5	6
Day, Esq. ...	22	15	0	Rick O'Donnell, M.D.	2	5	6
For self ...	5	13	9	Fran. M'Gillycuddy	2	5	6
William Ponsonby,				Pierce Chute ...	2	5	6
Sheriff ...	11	7	6	Wm. G. Fuller ...	2	5	6
Samuel Morris, for				Thos. Jo. Quill ...	2	5	6
Man. Fitzgerald,				John Neligan ...	2	5	6
Esq. ...	11	7	6	James Connor ...	2	5	6
Ral. Marshall ...	11	7	6	M. Lawlor, sen. ...	2	5	6

	£	s.	d.		£	s.	d.
Rowland Bateman ...	11	7	6	J. O'Flaherty, jun....	2	5	6
Arthur Herbert, Col-				J. Jeffcott, M.D. ...	2	5	6
lector ...	11	7	6	Edward Dunne ...	2	5	6
Edward Denny ...	11	7	6	Wm. J. Crump ...	2	5	6
John Bayly ...	5	13	9	John Saunders ...	2	5	6
Samuel Morris ...	5	13	9	William Neill ...	2	5	6
R. Chute, Chute-hall	5	13	9	Jo. Blennerhassett...	2	5	6
John Blennerhassett,				Con. O'Leary ...	2	5	6
Clerk ...	5	13	9	James Day, Clerk ...	2	5	6
Anthony Denny ...	5	13	9	John Busteed ...	2	5	6
E. Denny, Captain				Wm. Collis, Captain			
True, and Clan.				44th Foot ...	2	5	6
Yeomanry ...	5	13	9	Rick O'Connel, Lieut.			
Robert Hickson ...	5	13	9	89th Foot ...	2	5	6
Rowland Bateman,				George Chute ...	1	2	9
jun. ...	5	13	9	Jo. L. Fitzmaurice...	1	2	9
Richd. M'Gillycuddy	5	13	9	G. Cashel, jun. ...	1	2	9
George Rowan ...	5	13	9	T. Pembroke ...	1	2	9
John Weekes ...	5	13	9	Js. M'Carthy ...	1	2	9
Thomas Quill ...	5	13	9	T. Fitzgerald ...	1	2	9
Edward Collis ...	3	8	3	William Walsh ...	1	2	9
Wm. Wilson ...	3	8	3	Theo. Bolton ...	1	2	9
Jer. King ...	3	8	3	Jer. Sullivan ...	1	2	9
Jas. Ch. Hickson ...	3	8	3	W. Tottenham ...	1	2	9
Daniel M'Gillycuddy	2	5	6	Hugh Donovan ...	1	2	9
George Cashel ...	3	8	3	J. Lynch, c.m.t. ...	1	2	9
Jas. Sheehy, M.D....	3	8	3				

The murder of the soldier on guard at the Custom House,
Tralee, was one of the few outrages committed in Kerry during
the Rebellion. It caused at the time a great sensation in the
county, and was talked of for years afterwards as a most atrocious outrage. The murderer was never found out.

This account corresponds exactly with that given to me by
persons who were witnesses of the man's death. The Custom
House was on Stroughton-row (before the one in Strand street
was finished by Judge Day), and occupied the two first houses.

The soldier was shot on the footway between the Custom
House and Dan Lee's gate, as it was then called. The sentinel
was heard to challenge, and immediately after a shot was heard,
and a cry of murder. The guard from the old jail turned out
at once when they heard the shots. The man was mortally
wounded in the femoral artery. He was a married man, and

the scene at his death, when his wife came to him at the Custom House (for they did not remove him farther), was most heartrending. He was a Protestant, and was attended by the clergyman of the parish. He stated to the last that he was fired at by a person in woman's clothes; but for what reason he was shot could never be guessed at, as the town and county, notwithstanding the hatching of the Rebellion was at that time going on, was very quiet, and no attempt at robbery was made at the Custom House, either then or subsequently.

REBEL COURTESY.

I am also indebted to Lieutenant-Colonel A. Montgomery Moore, of the 4th Hussars, for the following copy of a letter received by his grandfather, Lieutenant-Colonel Montgomery Moore, from the commander of the rebel army in 1798, when in command of the Royal Tyrone Militia at Cork :—

"Mountain Camp, 20th Sept., 1798.

" SIR,—The fortune of war having put your miniature in my possession, I have the pleasure of restoring it to you, by sending it to Mr. Swinney's, Dame-street, the place probably intended.

" The envelope was mislaid by my secretary before I had seen it; you will therefore excuse me not sending it with the original direction. However sanguinary the war has been carried on at your side, I cannot forget the respect one soldier should entertain for the property of another, particularly when a lady joins the claim.

" When you write on a similar or private occasion, if your name be legible near the seal, the letter shall be forwarded without other examination, if it fall into the hands of any party of our army; but I enjoin you, on your honour, not to allow your name on any official letter, nor to make use of mine, to my prejudice, at a future period.

" I have the honour to be,

" MACMAHON.

Nath. Mont. Moore, Esq., M.P.,
Lieut.-Col. Tyrone Regt., Cork,
or elsewhere.

Printed by Alexander Scarlett, Bridge-street, Omagh.